BLUE DAY

BLUE DAY

WEMBLEY '97:
THE HEROES' STORIES

By Richard Godden

First published in Great Britain and Ireland in 2017 by
Trinity Mirror Sport Media, PO Box 48, Old Hall Street, Liverpool, L69 3EB.

www.tmsportmedia.com
@SportMediaTM

Trinity Mirror Sport Media is a part of Trinity Mirror plc.
One Canada Square, Canary Wharf, London, E15 5AP.

1

Hardback ISBN: 9781910335642
eBook ISBN: 9781908319777

Photographic acknowledgements:
Getty Images, PA Images

Edited by: Harri Aston
Illustrations by: Ben Renshaw

Printed and bound by CPI Group (UK) Ltd, Croydon, CR0 4YY

CONTENTS

About The Author

Richard Godden is the deputy editor of Chelsea's official publications. Born in 1985, the Blues supporter has worked for the club since 2008, having previously written for *Calcio Italia* magazine. He has contributed to a range of official club books and was the ghostwriter for Bobby Tambling's autobiography *Goals in Life*. He lives in Surrey.

Foreword

When I was a kid, I wanted to be Chelsea's centre-forward scoring in an FA Cup final at Wembley, just as every young boy dreamed of doing, but that was never going to happen. *Blue Day* was the next best thing for me.

The woman who ran the press department at Warner Bros, where I was making records at the time, was a mad Chelsea fan called Barbara Charone. An American lady, Barbara was more fanatical about Chelsea than any English person I've ever met. When we're 4-0 down with 10 minutes to go, which thankfully doesn't happy very often nowadays, she will be the one saying: "Come on – we can do this!" And she means it.

She said this guy called Mike Connaris had sent in this demo of a song that he thought might be nice to bring out for the Cup final. I was just a bit reticent about doing a football song because they can be a bit naff – more have been naff than haven't over the years and, let's be frank, in the history of FA Cup final songs there haven't been too many that have stood the test of time.

"Just have a listen to it and see what you think," she told me. So I did. And it was the most fantastic song. It was a clear perspective of what life was like as a fan, and in particular for someone who supported Chelsea: the only place to be every other Saturday; have a drink, have a moan. It said everything that the majority of the FA Cup songs never did. So I thought, why not, let's just give it a go. Even without the Chelsea connotations, I could say that I would be proud to sing this song. It just went from there after that. At the same, you don't want to put a curse on things either. You start thinking, "What if we don't win it?"

Mike is a fanatical Chelsea supporter and he was thrilled to pieces that we were doing the song and we were able to get the team to come and sing along as well. I've usually kept it quite vague when people have asked me about who wrote the song and all that, so I really should give him and Barbara some credit! They were the driving force.

We got into the studio and everything was sounding great – and then we got the team along to sing the choruses! People like Gianfranco Zola and Gianluca Vialli had no idea about doing an FA Cup final song. These are cool dudes from Italy more accustomed to strutting about in Armani suits, and here we've got them jumping up and down shouting "Chelsea, Chelsea!" They were completely bemused, but in the most charming way, because Dennis Wise is such a disarming person. He made sure we had a real laugh.

We had a really jolly afternoon together and Dennis was on particularly good form. He was still in the process of 'teaching'

Gianfranco Zola English, which meant every other word was a swear word. It was pretty clear he'd have to adapt the language Dennis was teaching him. It was a lovely afternoon.

Then we did the video and a lot of it was shot at the old training ground in Harlington, which is like a whole different world to where the club trains these days in Cobham. My left arm was in a cast as I'd broken my elbow while I was skiing. Well, I'd like to be able to say I was skiing, but I was actually just standing there on my skis outside the hotel when I fell over sideways. At that time, I was doing a programme called *Night Fever*, which was this crazy karaoke show which went out on a Friday night. We used to record four shows over a weekend because sometimes the same guests would appear back to back, but then they would stagger the shows to make it look like we had more guests than we actually had. So, one week I had a cast on, then the next it was off, then back on again. The letters were flying in!

At the end of the music video, the players were all taking it in turns to say, "It's gonna be Blue." Every time Vialli went up to the mic to say it, something would go wrong. That was all Dennis Wise! He got in the control room and he said, "We're only messing about, we'll do it properly this time" and every time Luca went to sing he would do something else. They were a good humoured bunch.

If you look closely enough in the music video, you can see me nutmeg Mark Hughes. I can say with some degree of certainty that moment was the highlight of my entire life. It was just a great laugh, and it was clear they were more than just a great group of players – this was a great group of people. They were all on good form.

Like the majority of you reading this, I'm just a fan of

Chelsea Football Club and one thing I was always a bit wary of was meeting footballers, because it's like that thing about not meeting your heroes as it will always be a letdown. This wasn't. So many different characters and just a very exciting group of players and fellas. What a tremendous way to spend a couple of days.

We actually got into the charts with the song and were offered the chance to go on *Top Of The Pops*, but Ruud Gullit wouldn't allow the players to do it, which was a big disappointment for all of us. That would have been a lot of fun. But with this being in the build-up to an FA Cup final, he wasn't keen on his players hanging around with dodgy rock stars like me at the BBC before such a big game!

Three years earlier I had been at Wembley for Chelsea's first FA Cup final for 24 years, which was against Manchester United. I left with the Blues trailing 3-0 and just sat on the coach all on my own, waiting for everyone else to get on. The last thing I saw as I got up to leave was Glenn Hoddle getting himself ready to come on, taking his tracksuit bottoms off. Great player that he had once been, he was never going to get us three goals back.

When we eventually headed home, I remember us passing a coach-load of Man United fans who were, quite rightly, celebrating and humiliating us. When 1997 came around, I had this horrible feeling again, even though it was Middlesbrough in the final and not the mighty Man U.

The day itself was just tremendous. The weather was beautiful, as it should be on FA Cup final Saturday. I'd actually hidden my jacket, which had my Cup final ticket and £200, in the airing cupboard the night before. I just thought that if there was ever a moment me and the missus were going to have a row, it's not going to be tonight and she tears up my ticket!

I had some friends, the Lays, who were working at Nine Elms, the Vauxhall vegetable market, and they were big Chelsea fans. They work all night and they were having a party at 8.30am. I left the house about an hour before that and the first thing I saw was a milk float with a big Chelsea flag on it, which was a good sign. I got down to their warehouse and they'd had two tonnes of sand delivered, so they had this kind of desert island and there was a steel band playing. Everyone was drinking cocktails and wearing Hawaiian shirts at 8.30 in the morning! It really was a sensational scene. We had a lovely old morning and I'd arranged an open-top double-decker bus. As we pulled away, somebody fell off the top deck, but fortunately he landed in the sand! I'll always remember someone else shouting: "Never mind how he is – just get his ticket off him!" It wasn't funny really, but he survived and he was able to watch the Cup final, which was obviously the most important thing.

I remember getting to the ground and everyone had celery, but people were being arrested for having stalks of it in their pockets! How the times had changed from when I first started supporting the club. It was hilarious. And that very rude song about it was being sung by everyone and the BBC desperately tried to talk loudly over it.

When the game itself finally got under way, I knew we had the better team and even though there was more expectation on us than there had been in 1994, any nerves disappeared when Roberto Di Matteo scored so early and it was just such an enjoyable game to watch.

It was just an unforgettable afternoon. To be honest, in the intensity of the game itself and willing the team to win, I'd completely forgotten about the song. That was the least of my worries, but I suddenly had this thought, "I've done that song – I wonder if they'll play it?"

When we won, this woman jumped on my back and she said, "You've helped us do this!" And then my seat collapsed, as did the seat in front of me, and we all ended up in a big heap. Then they started playing the song, and I cannot begin to tell you how proud I felt. It's one of those amazing feelings you never forget.

Then they played *Blue Is The Colour*, which is my favourite, before they played *Blue Day* again. At that point, all the other lot went and there were just Chelsea fans left in the stadium and it was one huge party. Then they played it again and again! It was one of the highlights of my entire life – one of those moments when you can't imagine anything getting any better. It was euphoric, up there with some of the greatest things I'd ever done with Madness. It's only if you're a football fan that you realise the enormity of these things. When that woman said to me, "You helped us do this", I'd never felt so proud in all my life.

I've been a Chelsea supporter for as long as I can remember. I lived in Fulham until I was about seven or eight, which is around the time the Kings of the King's Road team were coming through. I actually went to the same primary school that Alan Hudson attended! I was only a kid, but once you've decided, that's it. I can still name the first Chelsea team I saw – we had the five H's: Hudson, Harris, Hollins, Houseman and who's the last one? Marvin Hinton!

Then we moved to north London and I spent 27 years of misery being surrounded by Gooners! I had to put up with the whole George Graham period, 1-0 to the Arsenal, you might as well go home if they scored. And then out of the other side of that came all that glory. My daughters started to go with me before they discovered boys and now my nephews, who are in their late teens and early twenties, go with me and the generation game continues. For them, they think we should be winning something every season, because that's all they've ever known. But the darker days...

I used to go to every single game, home and away, in the early-mid Seventies, between the age of about 12 or 13 and 16 or 17. It was a very interesting period because we were going up, we were going down, we were going up, we were going down! The great thing about going down, as horrible as it is, is the moment when you start looking as though you're going up again. It's that thing about being 'back'.

When I was a kid, I would always watch games in the Shed. I think of that song by Slade: *Come On Feel The Noise*. I remember Noddy Holder talking about that idea of "feeling the noise" and when you were stood together, clapping and singing, it really did give you something that you can't really get when you're sitting down, which I sort of miss.

I've always liked the flair players, to be honest. Hudson was my hero at school, and Charlie Cooke. I loved Peter Osgood as well because he was a goalscoring machine. I just loved that team, basically. I'd been brought up on the 1970 FA Cup final team, but the guys in 1997 just took it up another notch. It was the sort of team that could win 3-0 one week and then go and lose by the same scoreline the following Saturday. It was that kind of excitement, it was intuitive football and really wonderful to watch. My barber is Sardinian and he used to say to me: "If Zola turned up and there were no floodlights, he'd still light up the whole ground." That's how it felt when you saw him on the pitch. He's up there with our very best. He's such a charming, humble, beautiful person as well. I had the great fortune to meet him a couple of times.

The other thing about that team was that it was so unexpected. I love watching Eden Hazard play, but we've become so used to seeing players of that quality at Stamford Bridge in recent years and there are no real secrets before a player signs – you've either already seen them in the Champions League or someone has put their best bits up on YouTube. Back then, there was an air of mystery about players like Zola.

We're shopping in the finest department stores nowadays, but back then it was almost like rifling through a jumble sale of players, hoping to get an item that didn't have too many holes in it! That was the start of an era when all these brilliant foreign players were coming over to these shores, it was a revolution.

I loved hearing all that rubbish about how "they won't like going up to Newcastle on a cold December night", which was just a load of nonsense – as if it's never cold in Italy. These guys came over and worked just as hard, they got stuck in and they became part of our club. Zola never drooped, he was never not bothered about a game – he loved football and he loved Chelsea.

There was a feeling that this wasn't just going to be a one-off and that something special was happening at Stamford Bridge. We were building a team, not just signing a few showboating, over-the-hill superstars. That whole team around Zola – the likes of Vialli, Petrescu, Di Matteo – that was the sort of football I love.

I received a signed football from that team and I recently gave it to a mate of mine for charity. All of those signatures are completely indecipherable, it could have been anybody squiggling on it but I can assure you, if you're lucky enough to have won it, that it's completely legit. The only problem is that it's a little bit old, a little bit faded and a little bit flat – a bit like me! It needs a bit of pumping up and a bit of dusting, but not like the team at the moment. They're absolutely fantastic. We've become so accustomed to winning and I think that shows just how big a moment the 1997 FA Cup final was for Chelsea.

I'd also like to inform everyone reading this book that I own 1997 as far as this football club is concerned, not any of the players who made it such a special year for us. That is absolutely true. The club had a lovely do in the Butcher's Hook to celebrate its centenary and they were giving years out to various people. Dickie Attenborough got a year, I think Raquel Welch ended up with 1969 – I'll leave that to your imagination – but I don't suppose there was too much competition for that year. For '97 I had to fight off some really strong competition! It was another really special day in my life.

There has long been a link between Chelsea and ska music culture. I remember very clearly when they first used to play Liquidator in 1969/70 and it caught on at Chelsea then. Obviously, that was a great time for ska and reggae in Great Britain and it seemed to go down very well at Stamford Bridge. It's funny now to here that continuum through a song like Liquidator, which is played as the team walks out each game, and also through my song, *One Step Beyond*. It's a bit of a strange link, but a nice one for me because I have always liked that type of music.

I was there the first time they played *One Step Beyond* after a game, when we beat Barcelona, and what an amazing night that was anyway. It was amazement upon amazement and that spontaneous reaction to the song in the crowd, it was extraordinary and it has been since.

There is a banner at the ground now with "The Only Place To Be Every Other Saturday" written on it and I remember when Ken Bates built the West Stand they put, "Chelsea, Chelsea" across the seats, so the name was written twice, just like the chorus. It's tremendous and in the longevity of things, it's very nice to think that *Blue Day* will survive. *With One Step Beyond* and *Blue Day*, the connection with Chelsea fans is terrific. It's a privilege to see people jumping up and down to those songs.

Suggs, April 2017

Introduction

Chelsea began the final decade of the 20th century with a home game against Aston Villa on New Year's Day. Bobby Campbell's Blues side fell to a 3-0 defeat and later that month crashed out of the FA Cup against lowly Bristol City, an all-too-familiar feeling for the club's long-suffering supporters. Though the season ended positively, with a Wembley triumph over Middlesbrough in the final of the much-maligned Full Members Cup and a fifth-place finish in Division One, it was yet another false dawn.

Fast forward to the end of the Nineties and Chelsea were competing in European competition for the third successive season, never before achieved in the club's history and a milestone accomplished with a maiden voyage into the Champions League – the big time like we'd never known it before.

The decade concluded with matches against Southampton and Sheffield Wednesday, both of whom were taken on with an all-foreign starting XI, the first time an English club had lined up without a single domestic player. A few months later, Colin Hutchinson, the club's chief executive, declared: "We are a continental club playing in England." What a transformation it had been.

There were so many pivotal moments which led to the awakening of this sleeping giant. Starting with the short-term appointment of David Webb, who had been the match-winner in Chelsea's only previous FA Cup triumph, the club has only headed in one direction. Glenn Hoddle was at the heart of the root and branch reform that followed, backed by chairman Ken Bates and wealthy benefactor Matthew Harding, although the latter tragically died in a helicopter crash at the beginning of the season when silverware finally returned to Stamford Bridge.

By that time, the club had already signed Ruud Gullit and Mark Hughes, the start of a playing revolution which gathered pace as the decade progressed, and as the nation became gripped with the notion of Cool Britannia and football 'came home' at Euro 96, west London was soon the trendiest place to be every other Saturday.

When Chelsea returned to Wembley for the FA Cup final in 1997, having been hammered on a drab day at the home of English football by Manchester United three years earlier, it just felt like it was our time – that it was going to be a Blue Day.

I hope younger readers of this book, many of whom have only known Chelsea as a club which competes for the biggest honours in this game, are able to grasp the importance of this FA Cup win, which truly was a turning point in our history.

The club's fanbase boomed after our first FA Cup win in

1970, when a television audience just shy of 30 million – a figure only eclipsed in the UK by the World Cup final in 1966 – tuned in to see us defeat Leeds United in a brutal final replay at Old Trafford. But while there was rarely a dull moment in the 27 years that followed that victory, joyous occasions were few and far between.

That side, known as the Kings of the King's Road, is fondly remembered but was broken up prematurely without truly fulfilling its potential. Games were subsequently played out in a lopsided Stamford Bridge, the mammoth East Stand – which had been constructed at great cost and almost led to financial ruin – serving as a constant reminder of the heroes who had to make way in order for the club to continue to operate. Even then, had Clive Walker not scored a crucial goal at Bolton Wanderers' Burnden Park in the penultimate game of the 1982/83 season to help us avoid dropping into the old Third Division, it could have been curtains for Chelsea Football Club.

Despite all this, the Blues were still a big club; 20,000 supporters packed into the Clock End at Highbury to witness Kerry Dixon's equalising goal on our return to the First Division in 1984 would testify to that. Huge numbers turned out at Wembley for the two Full Members Cup wins, the club's only silverware, aside from Division Two championships, between 1971 and '97. But there was always a banana skin awaiting us around every corner.

Although it would be rewriting history to say it has always been plain sailing since Dennis Wise lifted the FA Cup in 1997, since then the Blues have not finished lower than sixth in the Premier League and have won every major honour at least once. Beating Middlesbrough was the first chapter of a success story which shows no signs of ending.

It should be noted that this book is not intended to be the definitive story of that triumph. There are, of course, plenty of tales from the season included within, but the campaign has already been covered in great detail by the club's official matchday programme and magazine, as well as through the fantastic *Blue Days* podcast. A book may have allowed for more detailed coverage but, as memories become a little hazier 20 years after the event, ultimately it would have gone over the same ground and become very repetitive.

I was 12 years old when this Chelsea side made history and it was the first taste of success I had enjoyed as a football supporter. These players were my boyhood heroes and I wanted this to be about them, a platform to not only tell their stories, but also the story of the football club throughout a decade which gave the supporters so many incredible memories.

The manager and each of the men who stepped onto the Wembley pitch on Saturday 17 May 1997 have been given their own chapter and, such was the make-up of the group, it has made for a pretty eclectic mix of tales.

Steve Clarke was the natural starting point for the book as he had been part of the last Chelsea side to drop into the second tier, which made him the player who was best placed to discuss the subsequent rise under Glenn Hoddle and beyond. That he worked as assistant manager under José Mourinho when the club stepped up another level simply added another layer of context to his story.

Dan Petrescu and Mark Hughes were two of Hoddle's best acquisitions; one at the peak of his powers, the other coming to the end of his career, but both sharing the winning mentality that needed to be added to the mix at that time.

I was genuinely surprised by the latter, who proved the old adage of not judging a book by its cover. In the full glare of the media, Hughes appears to be a bit tetchy, but one-to-one he was engaging, funny and just a genuinely nice bloke.

Then there were the two homegrown youngsters, Eddie Newton and Frank Sinclair. Their friendship has lasted more than 30 years, which is roughly the length of time the former has been associated with Chelsea Football Club, give or take the odd spell here and there, and he was the most generous with his time of any of the interviewees, so much so that he almost missed Christmas lunch at our Cobham training ground!

Though he was clearly the life and soul of the dressing room, the chapter title of Fun Time Frankie doesn't really do justice to Sinclair. For all the fun he had off the pitch, he was a fiercely competitive character who managed to extract every ounce of ability from within himself. Both he and Newton were vastly underrated as footballers, but not by their peers. Both conceded penalties in the 1994 FA Cup final but retained the strength of mind to channel that experience to become Cup final heroes for the Blues.

Oh, Dennis Wise! None of this would have been possible without this straight-talking leader of men, who was the glue which held the group together. I first met Wisey at the club's Annual Lunch a few years back, when he took part in a Q&A on stage with three other great Blues captains: Roy Bentley, Ron Harris and John Terry. Four very different characters, but each contributed massively to the great tradition of the captain's armband at this football club.

The odd one out in our Cup final team was Frode Grodas, whose stay in west London was short but sweet. With this chapter, his time at the club was almost a secondary consideration and I felt there was more to be gained from his back story seeing as very little is known about this affable Norwegian chap. It was worth delving beneath the surface to reveal a complex character with a very dry sense of humour.

During the course of my interview with Clarke, he mentioned that Scott Minto was always a very conscientious individual and that has always shone through whenever I have interviewed him. He was the first person I spoke to for the book and after he apologetically cut short our chat to pick up his kids, he told me: "If you haven't got enough material, call me at any time."

Minto had some great stories to tell about Gianfranco Zola, who is every bit the gentleman everyone says he is. At one point he was the unanimous choice as the club's greatest player, though we have had a few more candidates emerging in recent years, and he is genuinely humbled by his standing among Blues supporters. I think the closest he came to boasting during the course of the interview was when discussing golf and his many victories over his regular playing partner and best mate, Kevin Hitchcock. As much as Zola and Co brought to English football, they remain eternally grateful that we introduced them to drivers and irons.

Ruud Gullit's chapter begins in the club's training ground at Cobham, where he is the centre of attention on a rare visit to the club. Many of the current crop of players are too young to have seen him play but based on his achievements throughout his playing career, he is the biggest superstar in Chelsea's history, comfortably among the top 20 footballers in the history of the beautiful game. And he's great company. What a coup it was for the club to attract him at a time when

Chelsea was seemingly light years away from the club it has become today. The subsequent gamble to appointment him as player-manager simply accelerated that process.

After months of attempting to tie down Gianluca Vialli to an appointment, the Italian invited me to an impromptu meeting at his home in Chelsea, where I was greeted by his butler! He was every bit as charming as he comes across on television and I could have happily spent all day listening to him talk about football. Sadly, that prospect was not quite as appealing to him, but I won't hold it against him. And for those who recall the hoo-hah which accompanied the not-too-crafty fag he lit up in the tunnel at White Hart Lane, you'll be pleased to hear he has given up the tabs!

Some of the players interviewed for this book – most notably Roberto Di Matteo, who led the club to the Champions League in 2012 – later returned to Stamford Bridge in other capacities and were instrumental in the club winning the biggest honours in the game. Nothing, however, can compare to being in the thick of it on the field. As the great NFL coach Vince Lombardi put it: "Any man's finest hour, the greatest fulfilment of all that he holds dear, is the moment when he has worked his heart out in a good cause and lies exhausted on the field of battle – victorious."

Ultimately, as likeable and charming as they all are, their legacy is built around one Blue Day at Wembley. Each of them played their part in making Chelsea great again and kick-starting an era of success. And that's the brilliant thing about this book; we're remembering a wonderful team and its brilliant achievements while the next chapter of the success story is being written. I speak for every Blues fan when I thank them for giving us a club to be proud of.

1. Mr Chelsea

'I've always said the game that meant the most was winning the 1997 FA Cup final. The first major honour of my career at a very late stage, three years after I thought I'd blown the chance to win a trophy.'

It was the final Saturday in the May of 1988, and gravel flew through the air towards the away supporters in the old North Stand. The players had long since left the pitch, but the real battle had only just commenced at Stamford Bridge, the scene of carnage an all-too-familiar sight in English football at that time.

Amidst the chaos, it was almost an afterthought that Chelsea had just been relegated, defeated over two legs by a Middlesbrough side who would take our spot in the top division of English football, the first and last time two clubs swapped places at that level following a relegation/promotion play-off.

Steve Clarke was Chelsea's right-back in that game, the only surviving member of that side who made it to Wembley nine years later, and he is reminded of that dark day by an elderly supporter who has spotted him chatting to me at a pub in Ockham, which is nestled in the idyllic Surrey countryside. Far from the bright lights of London, this is Clarke's scene; you can picture him here sat by the open fire with only a pint and the Sunday papers for company, but on this occasion it is his choice of venue to share his recollections of a Chelsea career that spanned 11 years as a player and a few more as a coach.

He chalks off the relegation as "character building" and the fan shakes his hand and thanks him for the part he played in giving us a club we could all be proud of. No selfie request, no fuss – only respect. Just the way Clarke likes it.

By the time he hung up his boots, he had appeared in 421 matches for Chelsea, a tally which had only been bettered by three players. It took until his last 42 games to win a major trophy and then, like the old saying about London buses, another two came along. He would win a further five major trophies as a coach alongside José Mourinho. The best years of his career were given to this football club – his football club.

"You have the biggest affiliation with the club where you spent the most time as a player and, for me, that's Chelsea after 400-odd games," Clarke says. "When I think back to the relegation, the tough times, the struggling in the middle of the table, bottom at Christmas time under Glenn Hoddle, all those are defining moments in your love for a club.

"I loved my time coaching with Chelsea and managing other clubs, but you never replace your playing days, that camaraderie and that bond you have with team-mates. You take all those bonds, all those different teams, all those different characters, all the good times and bad times, and that's what shapes your love for a football club. That's what shapes me with Chelsea. That's why it is my club.

"It was a big bonus being a coach at the time when they won the league for the first time in 50 years, but the s****y journeys up to Walsall, winning at Old Trafford – and scoring an own goal there – the crowd singing your name; those are the moments I remember and that bond with the hundreds of players I was lucky enough to play with throughout my career. Those are the moments that make it your football club."

Had Celtic, the club his family supported, acted with a bit more haste, Clarke might not be telling this story today. He grew up in Saltcoats, a small town in Ayrshire on the west coast of Scotland, with a big family around him – two brothers and five sisters – and he lived around the corner from the nephew of Bobby Lennox, a Hoops legend and a member of the side dubbed the Lisbon Lions which became Britain's first European Cup winners, and there was a big connection with

Celtic in the town. Opportunities to visit Celtic Park with his dad and uncle were rarely turned down by the young Clarke, but his fondest days of watching football were to come at Kilmarnock, the club his older brother, Paul, represented with distinction for over a decade.

"I supported my brother, really," he says. "I wasn't a Celtic fan and I didn't support Killie, just Paul. We actually played against each other when I was starting out with St Mirren and he was winding down. I can't remember too much about the game, mind, but there was quite a lot of publicity. Well, publicity in those days was a bit different, just an interview and a picture in the local paper. I've got a cutting up in the loft somewhere. We'd have probably got a week on Sky Sports News nowadays! I don't remember the result, but he keeps reminding me he scored that night. I really don't remember it! But he was certainly someone I looked up to and aspired to."

Fortunately, he didn't follow his brother's path to the letter. Paul quit ahead of his 30th birthday, after arguably his best season at Killie, to take up a more lucrative job in the police force. The very thought that football could not compete financially must seem alien to younger readers, but it was a prospect Steve, the middle of the three Clarke brothers, had prepared himself for after leaving school, when he underwent an apprenticeship with Beechams Pharmaceuticals, working as an instrument technician.

"I spent four years playing football and working in a factory, which was a good grounding for me," he reflects. "I earned more in the factory than I did in football. My first wage with St Mirren, which was part-time, was something like £25 a week. Your apprenticeship topped that up and actually I was quite affluent for a young person in the west of Scotland in those days! I always had a bit of money but I gave most of it to my mum. She looked after it for me. I did the apprenticeship because you never know, and in those days football was not a career for life. You always needed to have something, but I probably wouldn't have gone back to the same job or the same industry. What the apprenticeship does is to show you've got a capacity to learn and to understand, and you take some paper qualifications out of it and say, 'Look, I can do that.' I'm reasonably well educated and I was never too worried about coming out of football and going into something else, I would have found something. But I didn't really want to come out of football."

Clarke's father, however, had serious misgivings about him embarking on a full-time football career.

"He didn't see it as having any future at all, beyond your playing career. I'm quite stubborn, as most people that know me would say, and I decided that's what I was doing. To be fair, my dad backed me 100 per cent once I decided and he knew I wanted to do it. It's important, if you want to get somewhere, that you have the mindset that you're going to go out and do it. At that stage I had that. I went full-time, played another couple of years at St Mirren and then I got the call to come down here."

Celtic were also vying for his services at the time but, once the Blues expressed an interest, Clarke was quick to agree a move to London.

"I was linked with going to Celtic a lot," he says. "But they were messing around a bit with the money and Chelsea came in, made the offer, and I just thought I'd had enough of the Scottish Premier League at that time. I had no agent. I don't even recall asking anybody for advice. St Mirren said they'd accepted an offer from a London club, didn't even tell me who, and asked if I wanted to speak to them. I went round the corner to a hotel at Glasgow airport and John Hollins, who was the manager at the time, and Ken Bates were there. We had a quick discussion and I signed. Done. That was it. I went out, phoned my wife and said, 'Pack your bags, we're going to London.' She didn't know whether to believe me or not!"

By rejecting Celtic, he wasn't quite turning down the chance of healthily furnishing a medal collection which hadn't been added to since his days as a schoolboy footballer – though the Hoops won the title in what would have been his first season at the club, Scottish football was embarking on a decade of dominance by the blue half of Glasgow. But he had high hopes for Chelsea, despite the struggling First Division club he joined at the time.

After bouncing back to the top flight at the first attempt following the play-off defeat to Middlesbrough, the Nineties had actually begun with a fifth-placed finish in Division One under Bobby Campbell, albeit with the Blues closer in points to the relegation zone than champions Liverpool. Twice we breached the £1 million barrier to sign midfielders Dennis Wise and Andy Townsend, sparking hope of a return to the days when Chelsea could compete with the finest clubs in the land. It proved to be a false dawn and Clarke went through his unhappiest period as a Blues player in the months that followed.

"Bobby wasn't my favourite manager," he admits. "I didn't have a good relationship with him and, in fact, he's probably the only manager throughout my whole career where I can say I didn't have any kind of relationship with him. It was quite simple: he left me out! That's the bottom line. If you're a player and the manager doesn't select you, you tend not to like him. If he doesn't select you and doesn't give you any reason for not selecting you, doesn't explain or justify his decision, ignores you completely and treats you poorly, then you like him even less. That was the situation with me and Bobby. Eventually I asked to leave.

"Gareth Hall was keeping me out of the team at that time. I liked Gareth, he was a good guy, but I knew deep down in my heart that I had more to offer the team than him. He always gave 100 per cent and he did well for the club but, for me, it was always something I looked at and I couldn't work out in my head why I wasn't in the team at that stage. It's all part of growing up. I tucked it away in the memory banks and vowed not to be like that if I ever became a manager. The thing is, managers always come and go. I remember having that conversation with Bobby himself. It didn't go down at all well!"

Ian Porterfield, who had worked under Campbell briefly as a coach before returning to management with Reading, was chosen as his replacement and there ensued a summer of upheaval. Among those coming into the club were Paul Elliott and Vinnie Jones. Big voices in the dressing room. Clive Allen and Tony Cascarino followed during the season.

"It was a strong dressing room at that time, but there have been quite a lot of strong dressing rooms in the history of Chelsea, including in recent times. You need that. Ian tried to nurture the dressing room and get the team going. I got on great with him, he was a good friend and when he left Chelsea we kept in touch. He was always a good man and a good coach, but maybe not quite as good a manager.

"This is nothing to do with Ian, but I remember after training we'd all park up by one of the side streets at the end of the road and there was a bus where you sat down and had a greasy breakfast or greasy bacon roll. If it wasn't that, it was the pub. We'd have a liquid lunch on Tuesday. It sounds horrendous now when you talk about it, but it's what you did in those days. It wasn't just Chelsea, every club was doing it. That was how it was."

Dave Webb provided the shot-in-the arm the club needed when Porterfield became the first manager to be sacked in the Premier League era, but giving the hero of our 1970 FA Cup final win over Leeds United the job on a long-term basis would not have been the right call, however much the fans may have wanted it. To do that would have been to dismiss the mistakes of previous years and continue doing the same thing over and over, but expecting different results.

While there was no obvious upturn in our fortunes in the league under Glenn Hoddle, where we continued to hover around mid-table, there were long cup runs to galvanise the playing squad and the fan base. More importantly to the long-term development, there was a sense of purpose to what was being preached, a clear direction.

"In the early days at Chelsea, or even at St Mirren, there wasn't the depth of coaching or preparation for matches," he recalls. "You just trained to stay fit. You played football in training, did some crossing and finishing drills, attack v defence, but there was no real emphasis on, 'This is what we're doing and why we are doing it, this is how we're going to be better than the opposition on Saturday.' Nothing like that in the early days.

"On the training pitch, Glenn was the one that started planting little seeds about coaching and looking forward in the game. I was getting older and thinking, 'Do I want to go back to the factory or do I want to stay in football?' From that little period of time with Glenn, I started thinking about my future in the game, about coaching, working in the game. I was just about to turn 30, which is the time you started thinking about that. Back then, if you got to 35 as a player it was a long career. I almost made it, but not quite. So it was good for me that Glenn came in.

"What triggered the thinking a little bit was playing a completely different system, the 3-5-2. We'd touched on it a couple of times with Bobby Campbell – he tried it at Bristol City in the cup and we got absolutely smashed. I remember the night before we had a meeting and he demonstrated the formation on a Subbuteo pitch. Graham Roberts kept jumping in and saying, 'What if he goes there, or what if he goes here,' and he kept moving the players. In the end it was just a mess of Subbuteo players on a table. We played like that the next day.

"When Glenn came in, I'd got myself into really good shape for his arrival, I was super fit. I used to always be at the back of the running group, but that summer I was near the front. I pushed myself to be as fit as I could be because I wanted to be in the team. New manager, new chance. It worked out quite well for me and from there I went from strength to strength. I got Player of the Year in his first season and that bad spell I'd had over the previous couple of years was what I needed to push me on to find another level that I maybe didn't know I could find."

The general consensus within football is that the most prestigious awards are the ones voted for by the players themselves, but that is not an opinion shared by Clarke. The view of the supporters is something the Scot paid heed to throughout his time at the club, and he remains in contact with a few of the fans he became friendly with during his playing days.

"When I was scouting, I always tried to listen to the crowd, particularly the locals," he recalls. "If you're watching a player and the crowd likes him, it tells you that he's a good player even if he's having a bad game when you've come to watch him and you think he's not very good. Those people who go to watch every week are the ones who, normally, are a good judge of a player. They understand.

"It meant a lot to me for the Chelsea fans to choose me as their Player of the Year. Throughout this interview you'll get an understanding of how frustrated and disappointed I was with previous seasons, where I felt a lot of things had gone against me; I was never quite fit, never quite happy with the management, never really involved in the team for a regular run of games. I came back that pre-season as fit as I've ever been and with the feeling I was going to give it everything I've got that season. To be rewarded at the end of it was just a little vindication for all the hard work and effort I put in to get myself right and back in the team.

"I'd changed my game and adapted for the better. When I came down it was as an attacking full-back. Then some managers decided I'd be best curbing my attacking instincts and being a little bit more defensive. So that's what I did. I was never a player for pushing myself forward for personal glory or headlines. I just wanted to be part of a good team. Eventually I managed to do that. It took a bit of time..."

Under Hoddle, Chelsea reached the 1994 FA Cup final and the last four of the European Cup Winners' Cup the following year, and more money was also being invested in the squad.

"Looking at the wider picture, Glenn was obviously the catalyst for what was to come, as we started to attract bigger and better players," Clarke continues. "But I think you have to give a lot of credit to Ken Bates and Colin Hutchinson because they saw the way the game was going and they wanted to make sure Chelsea was on that path. They started to spend the money. And they backed Glenn even when we were really struggling under him. He wouldn't have made it to Christmas in his first season if it was in the modern game. No chance. Out the door.

"He got us thinking a bit more. I remember before the European games we'd get a little rundown on the teams we were playing so we'd have a better idea of them. Slowly, the tactics and the more in-depth analysis of the opposition came in in those days. Then Ruud [Gullit] got the job and didn't speak about the opposition again! But Luca [Vialli] was a little more thorough, he was a little bit more particular – I nearly said pedantic – in how he organised and got his team ready for games. Glenn's training was all with the ball, Ruud was the same, and Luca was more down the Italian methodology where you do a lot of work without the ball and then some tactical work with the ball. But not so much – it was more the fitness regime, getting yourself super fit."

An ability to change with the times meant that where others struggled with the changes and fell by the wayside, Clarke improved and thrived as part of the new continental Chelsea. He embraced the culture which was developing at the club and was handsomely rewarded with silverware.

"I thought it was great when all of these big names were coming in, it was a challenge," he says. "You could either give up, say they were better than you were and move on to another club, or knuckle down. I felt I had qualities that could help the team. That was always my idea. My qualities could complement what these guys were bringing into the club. I'd been there a long time and I could be a little conduit for them to come in and settle into the club, along with a lot of help from Wisey and various other people. I think the one thing that helped us settle as a group was that we made them come and adapt to us. We didn't try to adapt to them, although we took their good habits on board. We'd go out for a meal and you'd be sitting with the British boys all there with a pint of lager and they'd be there with a glass of water. You'd look at that and think, 'Okay – maybe you don't need a pint of lager every time.' Just those little things.

"I was at an age when I had to change anyway – in your early thirties you can't do what you did when you were 20. You have to change your lifestyle, your diet, the way you work. I was prepared to do that because I could see good things happening for Chelsea and I wanted to be part of it.

"When you think of the players who came in and lifted the place, they all adapted to us as much as we did to them. Ruud was a big, big star but he didn't act it. He wanted to be one of the boys, to settle into the group. He took us that little bit higher, up to a better level, and all these players coming in were always pushing us up another level, which eventually led to some silverware. Ultimately, that saved the club. If the club hadn't gone the way it had at that time, they'd have been left behind."

Throughout the interview, Clarke's facial expression rarely changes. His old team-mate, Michael Duberry, remembers this all too well from his days as a YTS lad, when he would cheerily greet the players in the dressing room and be met with little more than a grunt from one of the elder statesmen of the team.

"It was just me, just the way I am. I think a lot of people go out their way to be falsely polite, cheery and bright. But if I come in the morning and I've had a bad night's sleep or whatever and I don't feel like talking, I don't talk. But I think most people that know me would say I'm quite good company. I'm open and there's no agenda. I can look miserable – I've got one of those faces. Some people look happy and some look miserable. I've got the face God gave me and there's nothing I can do about it. That doesn't mean I'm not happy. But when you see me and I'm not smiling, I look grumpy but it's not always the case. Unless it was Doobs – then I definitely was grumpy to see him..."

The reality was a little different. Clarke was one of the silent leaders of the squad and he enjoyed working with the younger players, helping them find their way in the game. His influence may not have been spoken about in quite the same way as Wise's heart-on-his-sleeve style of captaincy, but it was certainly appreciated within the group and by the manager.

"He is as important to the team as Zola or Leboeuf or any of those type of players," Gullit said midway through the 1996/97 season. "Sometimes, players like Steve can be of more importance than the real stars. He has been outstanding for me and has also become a leader. You can see how he's worked at his game and he's given me his maximum. A quiet player who doesn't grab the headlines but the type you can always rely on. He tells players what to do, talks to them in a nice way and gets respect without having to shout and scream."

That season was Clarke's 10th full campaign at the club, his testimonial year, and the long wait for success made it taste all the sweeter when it arrived.

"I've always said the game that meant the most was winning the 1997 FA Cup final," Clarke says. "The first major honour of my career at a very late stage, three years after I thought I'd blown the chance to win a trophy. I knew I was coming to the end of my career, you can feel it. After the final in 1994, one of the coaches said: 'You've been here, you've had a taste of it. Bottle this feeling up and the next time you get to a final – and there will be a next time – remember how bad you feel and promise yourself the next time you get here you'll win it.' At the time, I thought his words were quite hollow. I'm thinking, 'Shut up, my time has gone and I'm never going to get another chance like this.' Fortunately he was right and I got a chance to go back."

It was an opportunity he almost missed out on. The flaring up of an old back injury meant he barely featured in the run-up to Wembley, and the final league game of the season was his last chance to prove his fitness.

"Where I'd broken the bone a few years back, a hairline fracture, when it healed it grew a little spike on it. In the weeks leading up to the Cup final, I almost never played. I couldn't even run. We were trying everything to find out what the problem was and my back was getting stiffer and stiffer. I hadn't played for a few weeks and then I went for a scan, a specific images scan, where they found the spike, which was digging into the sciatic nerve and causing me pain down the back and front of my leg. Eureka, this is what's causing it. I had to go into hospital and they gave me an injection in my back. It was laser guided, an MRI with an injection. They just put anaesthetic in. Got me to stand up, touch my toes. Perfect.

No pain, nothing. Clear. Phew. Before that, I'd been told I had to play against Everton on the final day or I wouldn't be considered for Wembley. I was going to play against Everton no matter what, but they managed to find the problem and it was great. The week before the Cup final, I went in for another of these injections and they put in cortisone this time, just to take the pressure off the area. I managed to play the final no problem."

At the time, we were on the second-longest run in the club's history without winning major silverware. It had taken us half a century to lift our first trophy, the 1955 First Division championship, which was followed by a League Cup 10 years later and then back-to-back FA Cup and European Cup Winners' Cup wins in 1970 and '71. A quarter of a century then passed with only two Full Members' Cups and two Second Division titles to show for it. Beating Middlesbrough meant so much more than *just* winning the FA Cup.

"It was a major step forward, something you felt was big for the club," Clarke reflects. "And it turned out to be that way because the club built on that success. Maybe if we hadn't won it and things had gone against us, the club would have gone in a different direction. You never know. It just felt like a really key moment in the evolution of Chelsea Football Club.

"I remember hugging Wisey at the end of the game, and I think we both said something like, 'That'll shut everybody up now. They can stop talking about the 1970 team.' I don't know, maybe it's just me, but you don't want to always be harking back to when you were a good team, having to remember when you did this, that and the other. You want the supporters to be constantly seeking success, not looking back to find it. Chelsea have got that now. They're not thinking about the

1997 FA Cup final or the 1998 European Cup Winners' Cup final, they're thinking about winning the league. Next season it will be winning the league, the Champions League. That is the evolution you want for your support.

"You want to remember the old days, but you always want the next trophy. People say Chelsea have got no history. Well, they have now. They're making history. In the last 20 years, it's a great history. In 20 years' time, hopefully they'll still be successful."

His time as a player at Chelsea didn't quite span the whole of the Nineties, as he departed in 1998, winning the European Cup Winners' Cup in what turned out to be the final game of his playing career. If it sounds like a romantic finale, it was anything but.

"It was a staged retirement," Clarke explains. "That summer I went with Luca and the other coaches to Bermuda, just a little break, and I was invited to join the staff. So I was to become player-coach the following season, which was telling me I was getting bumped out of the team. They brought in Chapi [Albert] Ferrer and Marcel Desailly, and I was looking as though I was just going to be a bit-part.

"On top of that, I actually struggled all pre-season with an injury and my options were quite simple: complete rest for anything up to six months, or an operation. There was no way I was having the op, which had serious long-term risks attached to it. Then I got a phone call – did I want to go to Newcastle with Ruud? I wasn't doing any coaching. It was just, 'Clarkey take the warm-up.' All the lads were looking at me, but Wisey was the one to say it: 'What are you doing?'

"I never played again. That was me finished. I went up to Newcastle, which was completely out of my comfort zone, something I like to do every now and then, just something completely different. It was a difficult group of players, very experienced, and they're not looking at me as a player, they're looking at me as a coach: What have you got? It was demanding, but enjoyable.

"Ruud didn't last very long. At the start of the following season he just handed in his resignation letter and left. 'What about me, I've moved my family up to the North-East?' 'You'll need to stay then,' he told me. And that was it."

However, he returned just after the turn of the Millennium in time to see Gianluca Vialli sacked.

"I saw out the rest of that season under Sir Bobby Robson and Chelsea invited me back as a European scout. I was looking for young players abroad. I didn't find any, mind, although I did tell them about Fernando Torres. I also watched Cristiano Ronaldo as a young boy, so it was a good crop of players I was watching.

"I knew Luca was in a little bit of trouble because Colin Hutchinson appointed me and told me to report to him. When I spoke to Luca, he said, 'No, report to me.' So I knew there was a little bit of friction between them at that stage, although I didn't realise it was as serious as it was. Not long after that, he was gone."

Clarke's spell as a scout was short-lived, as he went on to lead the youth team before stepping up to the first-team coaching set-up under Mourinho for the 2004/05 campaign, when the Portuguese manager led the club to our first Premier League title. That year, the club's centenary celebrations included a vote for the all-time Chelsea XI, a side in which Clarke occupied the right-back position. Were the vote to take place today, I wonder aloud if he would still make the team.

"Of course! Why not? I can't think of anybody that would take it off me! No, I was in the right place at the right time. We'd just won the league and I was assistant manager of a team doing really well, along with my big connection with the club. I was maybe top six in terms of appearances, but I've dropped a few since then. Whether I would get it again, I don't know, but it was a great honour to be selected in the team. I won't be around when they name the team for the 200th anniversary, so I don't need to worry about that one."

2. Super Dan

'Every day at the club was special.
It was everything for me, the best
time of my life as a footballer.
Every time I go to watch Chelsea
I feel like I am at home again.'

I am now in a position to empathise with the Premier League's left-sided wingers and full-backs of the mid-Nineties; Dan Petrescu is an absolute nightmare to keep track of. Football's deepest and darkest outposts appear to be the destinations of choice for a man whose 14 years in football management have taken him on a career path which currently reads: Romania – Poland – Romania – Russia – Qatar – Romania – China – Russia – Dubai.

Although I have a telephone number for Petrescu, it was for a mobile phone issued to him by Kuban Krasnodar and passed on to me by a member of their media department so I could interview him for Chelsea's monthly magazine a few years back. Incidentally, after this was published the club requested a copy of the magazine to put in their museum and it took pride of place beneath the Division One trophy Dan had led them to earlier that year. Frode Grodas suggests I speak with Tore Andre Flo, who joined the club shortly after our day out at Wembley in 1997, as he suspects he will have a number. And he does – two of them, in fact. Neither work. The next day I meet with Roberto Di Matteo and he too has a number. This one appears to work; it's ringing…

"Yes, this is Dan," comes the response of the deep, raspy voice on the other end of a crackly line. "I'm watching a game. Call me in one hour and I'll give you another number – a better one – to phone me on. I always have time to speak to Chelsea."

One of the biggest fears when foreign footballers were flooding into the English game in the mid-Nineties was that they were only in it for the money. Supporters in this country demand one thing above all else. Yes, quality is important, but more than anything we want the players to share our passion for the shirt, to show that playing for Chelsea is the most important job in the world. Petrescu and the first batch of overseas imports to join at that time all bought into that idea. They fell in love with Chelsea. For Petrescu, this adoration went far further than the hollow gesture of kissing the badge. He named his daughter after the club.

"Chelsea is very, very happy with this! Now she's in London at school. When people ask her name, people say to her, 'Really, you are the daughter of Dan Petrescu?' At first, no one believes her that my wife and I called her Chelsea. But she's happy. She says to me, 'Daddy, now I like my name more because everybody likes me here!' They are all Chelsea fans and there are a lot of them now."

That is thanks, in no small part, to Petrescu and his role in the Chelsea revolution of the Nineties.

The Romanian's move to England fit a familiar pattern at that time: impress at a major international tournament, sign for a Premier League team off the back of it. World Cups and European Championships effectively became a shop window for players representing smaller nations to shine a light on themselves and he had done exactly that for Romania at the 1994 World Cup, helping his side reach the quarter-finals before missing a penalty in the shoot-out defeat to Sweden. A flurry of foreign imports arrived in the Premier League following the tournament, with Petrescu among their number when he signed for Sheffield Wednesday. Chelsea's transfer business that summer saw us sign Paul Furlong for a club-record fee, followed by Scott Minto and David Rocastle. For all the advances being made under Glenn Hoddle, we remained a step behind.

A year later, in the summer of 1995, there was a meeting at

the Marriott Hotel in Langley, near Heathrow, which would change the course of Chelsea's history. The wheels had already been set in motion to sign Dutch superstar Ruud Gullit, although the deal was still to be confirmed, when Ken Bates, Matthew Harding, Colin Hutchinson, the chief executive, and Hoddle met up to discuss the bigger picture of that deal; not so much what Gullit could do on the pitch, but how his signing could shake up the image of the club and bring about a new philosophy for how Chelsea went about its business. As Hutchinson put it, we could either accept being a middle of the road team or to grab the bull by the horns; a decade later, the club had won the Premier League title.

Although Petrescu's subsequent move to Chelsea later that year wasn't exactly the type of signing that fit into the principles of the so-called Marriot Accord, it just made sense on every level. Unlike the other big names who had moved to the Bridge, he was only 27 years old and approaching the peak years of his career. He was, according to team-mate John Spencer, who finished as our top scorer at the end of that season, someone who raised the level of others around him. "The sign of a great player is one who takes good players and makes them better," suggested Spencer. "That is what I felt happened with guys like Dan Petrescu especially."

What's more, he brought with him vast experience from club, continental and international football without representing the usual gamble that would have to be made to sign such a player from overseas, for he had already acclimatised to the English game during a spell at Sheffield Wednesday. None of our other foreign signings could be classed as such a sure thing as Petrescu.

At the time, there was little to separate clubs such as Chelsea and Sheffield Wednesday. If anything, the Owls had more recent success to fall back on, and only two years previously they had finished as runners-up in both domestic cup competitions. But the Blues had two trump cards – prime location and a manager who was revered throughout the game.

"My first reason for signing was Glenn Hoddle," Petrescu reveals. "I always thought he was the main man in England. You must remember that Chelsea was not that much higher than Sheffield Wednesday at that time, but they showed me they were serious about building the club. I saw they wanted to change something, to do something special. Moving to London was also something I wanted to do, but I have to say it was mainly down to the manager. I knew him as a player and I was desperate to work with him. I also knew they'd signed Mark Hughes and Ruud Gullit earlier that year, so it was very good for me to see that they were at the club – it showed they were going in the right direction. So when Glenn called me and said he said he was interested in my services, I thought it would be a good move. And then they bring me and, afterwards, all the stars come to the club. Without the players you cannot make anything."

That last sentence was of vital importance when it came to identifying him as a potential signing. Yes, he lacked star quality; Paul Gascoigne had been one of the targets listed at the Marriot Hotel meeting, to give you some idea of the type of player the club was looking to sign, though they missed out on Gazza to Rangers. But even if he had signed, was he the missing piece in Hoddle's tactical puzzle? His creativity would have spruced up a workmanlike midfield, but we were missing something out wide. The manager's preferred 3-5-2 – or, as the papers tried to hype up Gullit's sweeper role, a

1-2-5-2 – system already featured one natural wing-back on the left-hand side in Scott Minto, although he spent much of the season injured, and a capable deputy in Andy Myers, but the same could not be said of the opposite flank. Steve Clarke had appeared there for some of his 1993/94 Player of the Year-winning campaign but, wonderful defender though he was and once a swashbuckling full-back in his heyday, the Scot was in the autumn of his career; Anthony Barness had struggled to make an impact since signing from Charlton; and Craig Burley, willing though he was, was a midfielder.

Dave Sexton, the only man to lead Chelsea to FA Cup glory prior to Gullit's appointment, rated Dan as the outstanding right wing-back in world football at the time and he took to the club immediately. Although his debut came in a defeat against Leeds, the 3-5-2 system clicked for the first time.

"Dan Petrescu has come and created chances straight away," said Hoddle just a few matches into his new signing's Chelsea career. "That is what is needed in this system. For Tottenham, Ronny Rosenthal was asked to man-mark Dan, and if you've got their left-winger marking your man you've got a good chance of going on the offensive."

And that was what it was all about at Chelsea, getting off the back foot and onto the front.

"It's no secret that I didn't like defending and preferred to go forward, and playing 3-5-2 allowed me to do that – it was the best for me," Petrescu says. "In this system you have cover with the three central defenders, which is what I needed. When I was in a four it was difficult for me to play right-back, I was going forward too much in 4-4-2. That is why, for me, Glenn was fantastic. He signed me as a wing-back – and you see Chelsea today playing with them again – he gave me the freedom and he always said to me: 'You are the best in the world in this position. You have to go forward all the time and enjoy yourself.' It was fantastic to have this freedom from him and to feel his confidence in me. He was very happy with me and, of course, playing under him was very good for me. Later, I moved into midfield and I had never played there before, but I adapted to it."

While it would be a stretch to say he became a regular scorer from midfield, he always chipped in with his fair share. Goals against Southampton and Tottenham Hotspur in 1997, in particular, highlighted the intelligent attacking play and deftness of touch which characterised his time in west London. On both occasions he saw space infield and drifted inside and, though the finishes would both be classified as lobs, they were very different strikes. For the first he ran with the ball from deep before executing a pin-point clip over the keeper from outside the box, followed by a typical Chelsea celebration as Di Matteo dropped to one knee to shine his team-mate's boot. The second was all about the timing of the run and the vision of Frank Leboeuf, who dropped the ball exactly into the space soon to be occupied by Petrescu. The volleyed finish, with the outside of his foot, was world class.

He appeared to take particular pleasure in scoring against Wimbledon, netting six of his 23 goals against the side from Selhurst Park, and he just seemed to have a sixth sense for space, whether coming late at the back stick, running in behind or hovering around the edge of penalty area. To play him at right-back would have been to deny the side a key attacking outlet, particularly in transitional phases, when his speed of thought and awareness truly came to the fore.

Additionally, he possessed the requisite European experience which had been patently lacking during our run to the Cup Winners' Cup semi-finals in the season before he joined, an achievement which should be lauded when you consider the players in our squad at that time. He was competing in the European Cup throughout his time at Steaua Bucharest. In a continental football landscape dominated by clubs from England, Germany, Italy and Spain, younger readers may scoff at the thought that a team from Romania could have been a dominant force, but in the late-Eighties Steaua were regularly competing, and succeeding, at the very highest level. He was a youngster at the club when they beat Barcelona in the 1986 European Cup final after a penalty shoot-out in which their goalkeeper, Helmuth Duckadam, saved all four penalties he faced to give his side an unlikely triumph against a club coached by former Blues midfielder Terry Venables.

"My childhood was only football," he says of life behind the Iron Curtain in communist Romania. "Every day, all day, just playing football. I grew up at Steaua and I love the club very much. I was born in Bucharest and, until I left Romania in 1991, I only spent one year as a footballer away from Steaua. My football life was there until I moved to Italy [to play for Foggia and Genoa]. Winning the European Cup was very important for Romanian football, but in that time Steaua was overall the best team in Europe. From 1985 to 1989 they reached the final of the competition twice and also the semi-finals twice. In the league we went over 100 games without losing. At Steaua we had an excellent team with good players and a very good spirit."

Steaua lost 4-0 to AC Milan in the 1989 European Cup final, when Petrescu came up against his future Chelsea team-mate and manager.

"Gullit played a very good game for them," he says. "They had the three Dutch players: Gullit, Marco van Basten and Frank Rijkaard, and they were unbelievable. They looked like they were from another world. And Gullit later became many things to me: my friend, my team-mate and even my trainer at Chelsea. Playing together in the same team with him, it was really like a dream. He was not playing any more in attack, but he was still a fantastic player, playing like a sweeper in the three defenders. Sometimes he went into midfield because he could be more effective. Whichever position it was, just playing alongside him was unbelievable. We became good friends and it was a great experience to work with him, but it was not so great to play against him in this European Cup final!"

Petrescu's experience proved vital in our memorable run to the European Cup Winners' Cup in 1998, although he missed the second-leg of our epic semi-final against Vicenza. The Blues trailed 1-0 from the first leg and conceded an away goal to the Italians before Gustavo Poyet, Gianfranco Zola and Mark Hughes struck to complete a magnificent comeback victory.

"The most important match for us was the one against Vicenza – the game I missed! That was unbelievable how that game turned in the second half. Normally when you play an Italian team, they score first and you cannot change the result, but Mark Hughes, Gustavo Poyet – unbelievable goals. I was sure it would need a miracle, because even though Vicenza are not a big club, they are an Italian team and they don't give you too many chances."

Petrescu was back for the final against VfB Stuttgart. Now, without wanting to paint too cruel a picture of the Romanian, he is right to say he was better going forward than defending because, with all due respect, he wasn't exactly fond of a tackle. But in Stockholm, with Chelsea leading 1-0 and time running out, he attempted perhaps the only hard challenge of his career and received a red card, becoming the first Blue to be dismissed in a European final. His reaction said it all – a pained look of bemusement.

"I didn't touch the guy," Petrescu insists, but it is not an incident he loses any sleep over.

"If you lose a game like this, it is a decision that you regret forever. But when you win, it doesn't matter about a red card, yellow card, score or no score. The most important thing is winning the cup. And for the club it was a big moment to lift a European trophy. The spirit we had was very good and it was a pleasure to play in that team. I feel very lucky. We were all friends, too, always doing things away from the pitch. You could see that from the way we celebrated our goals – everybody was enjoying the football. Enjoying the life. That will stay with me forever."

Ever the perfectionist, he was part of the new breed of dedicated professionals who were showing their English counterparts the way. He was regularly among the last in off the training pitch, but that wasn't the end of his day at Harlington. Gym sessions were an important part of his preparation, in particular yoga, which helped him immensely when a recurring back problem was threatening to get the better of him.

"Maybe everybody appreciated in my five years at the club that I worked a lot before and after training to make sure I was right," Petrescu says. "The football was different here and I had to adapt. Games were more aggressive, more difficult. In Italy you get a lot of fouls, it is a free-kick as soon as somebody touches you. Here there are no easy free-kicks. It was a while before I understood how it worked. But I was happy because it was football that I liked."

All that hard work paid off and he was able to enjoy so many fantastic moments at the club and he added three cup winners' medals to the four championships and two Romanian Cups he won in his homeland. But it's clear one trophy stood out above all others.

"Before I came to England, everyone said the most important thing was to play in the FA Cup final – and to win it – so when we did this against Middlesbrough I was very happy," Petrescu remembers. "It's not something everybody gets to do from my country. It was like a dream all the week before the final. It was different from a normal game, totally different. Even for me, I did not realise how big it was. Maybe that was better for me, because I didn't have too much pressure. But after I won it, I understood what it meant. Afterwards, everything was very good for the club, for this habit of winning. It was important the first one. I don't think we played a final and lost. All the finals we played, we won.

"And we never conceded goals in the finals, so you can see it was not only nice football we played. The mentality with Vialli was a little bit more defensive and under Gullit a bit more offensive. But with both of them, we had top-class defenders. Steve Clarke was one of the best defenders in the history of Chelsea, for sure. He is still a legend for Chelsea. I played three years with him – a fantastic professional and a great player."

Petrescu is glowing in his admiration of his former team-mates.

"There were so many fantastic players at the club: Vialli, Zola, Gullit, Hughes, Poyet, Di Matteo, Leboeuf, Desailly, list them all as I don't want to miss someone. I learned something from all of them. Dennis Wise was fantastic. He had so much energy and was a great player. And also a fantastic captain. I think as a coach I am missing a captain like him. He was a good motivator.

"All of them were good friends, as were all of the players at Chelsea. It was a good family at the club. But Gus Poyet was my best friend. We still speak now, he's still a good friend and I'm really happy to see him doing well as a manger. I helped him out with his English when he first came to Chelsea and that's how we became very good friends. It was not like this for me when I joined Chelsea, when John Spencer was my room-mate. He was absolutely crazy and really good fun. But his Scottish accent? I just couldn't understand it! Luckily, my English was better than when I joined Sheffield Wednesday."

Spenny has since carved out a coaching career for himself in America, where he played out the final years of his career, and if you go through the team line-up from the 1997 FA Cup final, Frank Leboeuf and Scott Minto are the only players who have not managed or coached anywhere since hanging up their boots. Some have gone on to enjoy huge success, most notably the pair of Roberto Di Matteo and Eddie Newton, who led Chelsea to Champions League glory in 2012. Many others have paired up, too. Frode Grodas and Erland Johnsen worked together at Lillestrom; Frank Sinclair joined Stoke City as Under-23s assistant coach under Mark Hughes; Steve Clarke briefly worked under Di Matteo at Aston Villa. If we expand the pool of players to those who joined in the 12 months after the FA Cup triumph, the Chelsea links continue: Gus Poyet and Dennis Wise at Swindon Town and Leeds; Gianfranco Zola and Pierluigi Casiraghi at Birmingham City.

"To be fair, I expected a lot of those players to become

managers – even Dennis! Then there's Zola, Mark Hughes, Di Matteo, me, so many others. Everybody should be managers because we were a very clever team. We played nice football, clever football, and I think any of us from that team can be good managers. I'm very happy for Gus because he was an assistant manager and I told him it was better to try on his own because he's a very intelligent guy – I knew he could do it.

"To see Robbie win the Champions League was incredible and I was supporting the club all the way. It was even more special for the players who were team-mates with him because we had big regrets after the quarter-final defeat to Barcelona in 2000, when we were all playing. We were only minutes away from going through at the Nou Camp. So, to see Roberto and Eddie Newton lifting this trophy was a good feeling for me. This made it more special."

Petrescu has also enjoyed success in his own managerial career, albeit on a smaller scale. Most notably he guided Unirea Urziceni to the Romanian league title in 2009, subsequently beating Rangers and Sevilla in their maiden Champions League group stage appearance. Then there was the afore-mentioned promotion with Russian side Kuban Krasnodar and more recently he won the Chinese equivalent of the FA Cup with Jiangsu Suning, who signed Ramires from Chelsea shortly after that triumph. I'm reticent to list Al Nasr in Dubai as his current club, for his track record suggests that will not be the case for very long.

Rather than following the lead of his three managers at Chelsea, each of whom enjoyed fleeting spells in the dugout before settling on television punditry, Petrescu appears to be following the example set by his first coaches at Steaua, Emerich Jenei and Anghel Iordanescu, who both enjoyed long and varied careers. He insists, however, that each of them acted as a role model in their own way.

"In my opinion, it was important for me to learn something from all of them," Petrescu says. "As a coach, you have to try not to copy anyone. This is my idea, I want to be myself. With Gullit it was a pleasure to go training. He was a friend, he was a coach, everything for me. He gave me a lot of confidence. I enjoyed everything. All the training was very nice, always with the ball and playing football. Not for a mistake did they say we played sexy football, because it was really like that. Gullit liked us to play football, he didn't like to defend, he wanted us to play all the time.

"I am more of a style of first not conceding a goal. But it depends on what team you have. You cannot go into a small team and say, 'Okay, let's play football like Guardiola plays.' It is just not possible. You need the players to play nice football."

What of Vialli, the manager who sold him in acrimonious circumstances? In April 2000, the Blues were beaten by Manchester United at Old Trafford, a game in which Petrescu scored and was later hauled off for failing to carry out his defensive duties. Instead of sticking around for the remainder of the game and rejoining his team-mates, the story goes that he showered, changed and headed for the nearest taxi rank. It proved to be the final appearance in Blue for our first overseas player to play 200 matches for the club and he didn't even make the bench for the FA Cup final.

"I left because Gianluca told me I would have no future at the club to play," Petrescu reveals. "I was sad because I had two more years on my contract and I wanted to finish my career at Chelsea. I didn't play too much in Bradford or Southampton after I left and the teams were not so good, so maybe I should have stayed. If he doesn't tell me this and he tells me to fight for my position, maybe I would have.

"Luca was good when he was a player, but when he became coach he had problems with me, Poyet and Zola. We were friends playing together. In this job, it's very difficult and you have to understand players. There is a difference between coaching and playing. He should have stayed friends with us. We told him, 'We respect you anyway, you don't have to do anything. We'll work for you, no problem.' Nothing else. He wanted to be tough, he wanted to be strong. But he lost all the players.

"We played fantastic also with him. He is not a bad coach. But he wanted to do it differently. In my opinion, all the work was done by Gullit. We were in the quarter-finals of Europe, semi-finals of the League Cup. Then Luca came in and we won the Cup Winners' Cup and the League Cup. Okay, he deserved some credit for both competitions."

Does he ever see himself writing another chapter in his Premier League story?

"I have coached in many countries and I think I have had success everywhere I have been. My dream is to come to England. Maybe one day it will happen, but if not it is just a part of life. I'm enjoying life – well, as much as you can do as a coach. It is another life, very different to being a footballer. I try to have success and hopefully one day I will get the chance to come to the Premier League."

So far, the closest he has been to the dugout at Stamford Bridge is while embarking on the traditional half-time pitch walk which has become a regular fixture at all our home games over the past few decades, featuring a beloved player from years gone by. Every time he takes to the field, you can see just how much it means to him. That same smile we saw so many times on that very pitch when he was playing, only this time accompanied by misty eyes.

"For me it's impossible to do this any more, there is too much emotion. I prefer not to be out there – I prefer to be in the stands like a fan. Spy [pitchside announcer Neil Barnett] always says, 'Come on, come on.' But I told him now I'm finished, no more. It's very difficult for me. I was very happy there and they know..."

He pauses. It's just like he is out on the pitch again, stopping to assess his options before picking the right pass; on this occasion he is searching for the correct words to sum up just what this great club means to him.

"You know, I have done many good things in my life and made many, many good decisions. For sure, signing for Chelsea was the best one. I loved my time there and if you asked me to pick one moment that I enjoyed more than any other, it would be very difficult for me. Every day at the club was special. Really, every day. Even now I still think of the good times I had with the club. I played in many games, scored many goals and we won some important trophies. We had one good year in the Champions League. But we never won the Premier League, which is maybe my only regret.

"Actually, I think I received something else that is more important. Every time I come back to London and the fans show how much they appreciate what I did for the club, this is the best thing for me – not how many games I played or how many trophies I won. It was everything for me, the best time of my life as a footballer. Every time I go to watch Chelsea I feel like I am at home again."

3. Sparky

'The challenge for me was
always the same: we've got to
make a mark; we've got to start
winning trophies again. That's
what happened at Chelsea.'

A trip up to Stoke City's Clayton Wood training ground is a journey into the unknown. Located just a few miles away from Stoke-on-Trent train station, it is not so much my destination which is giving me a case of the pre-interview jitters. Rather, it is the subject. Aside from the fact time is, understandably, of the essence for a Premier League manager, Mark Hughes has only a few days earlier witnessed his side knocked out of the FA Cup by Championship side Wolves. In the full glare of the media spotlight, the 53-year-old appears not too dissimilar from the on-field persona from his playing days: combative and with little inclination for niceties. The last thing he needs during the busiest period of the season is a sit-down interview two days before a vital trip to relegation-threatened Sunderland.

As the train reaches the Potteries, the temperature is noticeably chillier than London – six degrees cooler, BBC Weather reliably informs me – and the biting wind which sweeps across the train platform is soon, as I discover upon exiting the station, accompanied by a downpour of sleet. If Jeff Stelling and the gang were commenting on my progress, they would undoubtedly describe it as the ultimate test of a writer's credentials; the equivalent of the cold, wet and windy Tuesday night at the bet365 Stadium which, apparently, is the only thing standing between Lionel Messi and greatness. My nerves are not helped by a taxi driver who cannot find Clayton Wood, although he has my sympathies for it is tucked away down a small road at the back of a built-up residential area, but upon arrival I immediately feel the warmth of the club.

I wait in the small reception area which is chockablock with staff coming and going through the various doors which lead to a warren of narrow corridors, each of which is well known to its inhabitants but labyrinthine to outsiders. A familiar face pops his head around one of the doors. "Everything all right, mate? Are you being looked after?"

It's Eddie Niedzwiecki, one of Hughes's trusted lieutenants throughout his managerial career which, remarkably, is in its 19th year. Chelsea supporters older than I will remember Eddie as the goalkeeper who was a vital cog in John Neal's much-loved Division Two-winning side. He is also a former Player of the Year with the Blues, the third of five shot-stoppers to win the honour in the award's 50-year history, and a former member of the club's coaching staff after his playing days were prematurely curtailed by a knee injury in his prime. Indeed, he was the goalkeeper coach when the Blues lifted the FA Cup in 1997 and, as I am soon to discover, a key figure in his current gaffer's move to Stamford Bridge two years earlier. Or so he would have Hughes believe.

Then, bang on 2 o'clock, the scheduled time of our meeting, I am led up to a room which I had previously considered sacred, not to be entered by my kind: the manager's office. It has an informal feel about it and the huge windows allow anyone inside the perfect view of the training pitches below. Hughes is wearing a Stoke City tracksuit with the jacket zipped up as far as it will go, and as I walk in he is staring intently at the television, which is telling him Graham Taylor has just passed away. His gaze switches across to me and he offers his hand.

"It's a real shame," he tells me, referring to the former England manager. "I didn't know him well, but he was a nice guy. Anyway, what have you come to talk to me about today?"

Harlington, I inform him. Chelsea's former training ground is always a good ice-breaker with any of our Nineties contingent. A college sports ground located near Heathrow, there was little to like about the place, and its aged structure is in stark contrast to Stoke's recently redeveloped training facility in which our conversation takes place. There is simply no comparison.

"To say the very least," he begins, "and when I got there I think it had been markedly improved by Glenn Hoddle. The thing about it which didn't really work was there was all these little changing rooms with room for only seven or eight in each of them, which was okay but ideally it's not what you want to generate team spirit. In fairness, it didn't impact on the group we had. It was a good group. You may have thought it would be a problem.

"I can't remember off the top of my head who I shared with, but I know that when Luca [Vialli] came he was over in the corner of my dressing room. I was always next to the door. He used to sit in the corner and on his part of the wall he would put up little phrases to help him learn English.

"They'd only be little things he heard from others: 'But of course', or something like that, link phrases and so on. It must have worked because he speaks perfect English. You'd have a conversation with him and if he liked it he'd write it down and up on the wall it would go."

Chelsea only left the facility behind in 2005, moving to a soon-to-be state of the art training centre in Cobham, Surrey. Queens Park Rangers were the new tenants at Harlington and when Hughes took the job as manager, he was shocked by what he saw.

"The place didn't change for years and years, because when I got the QPR job I changed it all. That tells you everything. I thought, 'It can't be as bad as it used to be.' But I turned up and it was exactly the same, only 10 years or so older.

"There was always an issue with the pitches. We've got pitches here with undersoil heating and automatic irrigation and what have you, but we used to have to drag out a hose pipe ourselves. Pre-season was a nightmare, the pitches were bone hard. You'd be lucky to get one patch of grass with a bit of give in it. You just accepted it back then because it was the norm. It wasn't the exception. Now this is the norm. Different times, people had different mentalities towards it – you just got on with your job."

Since he was taking his first steps in the game, Hughes has only ever been out of football, by my crude calculations, for around 18 months. That is a hell of a lot of football he's experienced. He scored goals for four European Cup-winning clubs: Chelsea, Manchester United, Barcelona and Bayern Munich. He won league titles, domestic cup competitions – including the FA Cup on four occasions, which was a record for the 20th century – scored twice in a European Cup Winners' Cup final and was twice named PFA Player of the Year. He has managed his country, doing so for several years while still playing and almost leading them to the European Championship in 2004, and taken charge of a record-equal five clubs in the Premier League across more than 400 matches.

He also achieved what most fans reading this book dreamed of doing as a young boy: he played for the club he supported.

"I was a Chelsea fan," he confirms, "and they were my first main team, not Wrexham. A lot of my mates, all the same age, supported them too. I think there's a lot of 53-year-old Chelsea fans because of the 1970 FA Cup final. I was seven and that's an age when you first become aware that you should start following a team. They were in a Cup final, I quite liked the kit – and they won! So I thought, 'Yeah, I'll stick with them.' They were my first team and I know when I signed for Chelsea all my mates from Wrexham were delighted. I saw a lot more of them when I was a Chelsea player than I did when I was at Man United!

"But I never went to Stamford Bridge until I was a player, it was always from afar that I followed them. I was living in a little village in north Wales, so we didn't venture much further than the five miles to Wrexham. That was a journey for us. You were always hoping Chelsea were going to be on Match of the Day or chosen for the Sunday game. Or in the Cup final. That's how it was. But you'd buy Shoot magazine every week, which had the posters in it, and you were always longing for the team photo to be in there because that was a big deal if your team was in the middle of the publication."

The club he is currently managing caused a huge stir in their first Premier League campaign thanks to the freakishly long throws delivered into the penalty box by former schoolboy javelin champion Rory Delap, but long before that the Blues could boast the best in the business.

"I think my favourite player was probably Ian Hutchinson, simply because of his long throw," Hughes says. "In fairness, I don't actually remember too much about his style of play, it was just his unique way of throwing the ball. I used to try and do it in the playground, everyone was at it. He was double-jointed, so there was absolutely no way you could replicate it. Peter Osgood was another one because he was the main goalscorer and then there was Alan Hudson as well, who has obviously got the Stoke connection, too."

Hughes signed for the Blues in the summer of 1995, leaving a Manchester United side that had not long ended a 26-year-wait for a top-flight championship which went back to the days of Sir Matt Busby. Having won the title and followed it up with the Double, disappointment followed with a trophy-less season in 1994/95, during which the club signed the prolific Newcastle United centre-forward Andrew Cole to effectively replace Hughes. But then Eric Cantona attacked Crystal Palace fan Matthew Simmonds during a game at Selhurst Park, launching a kung-fu kick at him in one of the most shocking incidents ever witnessed at a football ground. He received a substantial ban for his troubles and Hughes was handed an Old Trafford lifeline.

"I was uhmming and ahhing about it," Hughes remembers. "I thought I wouldn't be playing much so it was probably time to move, but then Eric did that and I'm thinking, 'He can't come back from that. I might get a couple more years', and I actually re-signed for another two years. But then in the summer he told everybody he was coming back in September and I thought I was back in the same situation. The club was obviously clearing the decks, so I'm thinking, 'See what options there are.' Eddie tells the tale that I was speaking to him about all this when we were at Wrexham golf club. He rushed back, spoke to Peter Shreeves and Glenn Hoddle, and said, 'You might have a chance with Mark Hughes.' It kind of snowballed from there and I ended up going down there.

"They were talking about signing Ruud, that was part of the pitch about how they were trying to get better, and I knew I wasn't one of the main targets. I was out in America when I signed and we did it all by fax, as you did in those days and still do now to a certain extent. They did a big PR launch for Ruud coming and signing, top table and all that, and and then someone said, 'By the way, we're signing Mark Hughes as well.' I was stuck on the end, but I didn't mind that, I wasn't motivated by any publicity, it was just about getting on with the job and making the right move."

At United, Hughes was regularly competing for major honours, but now he faced a very different challenge – and one that he relished.

"The main difference between the club I was leaving and the one I was joining was that United were at the top of the pile and Chelsea were a mid-table team," he says. "That's what they were, basically; hadn't had a lot of success, hadn't really invested a great deal in the squad or at least in terms of the level of players they were looking to sign when Ruud and I came. But from my point of view it was a perfect move because I felt I still had more football in me. I was 31 when I left and I still felt I could play for four or five years, so I needed to pick the right team. Chelsea just made sense to me. There was potential there. It's always the same when you leave a top club. You don't want it to be seen as, 'That's it, you won't win trophies again and you won't be part of a top team, you're going to slide off the scale.'

"I still had a point to prove and that helped my focus for when I moved. But I always remember when I came back from America after I'd signed, I went to the stadium for a few publicity shots and they made me point towards the Matthew Harding Stand [then the North Stand]. That was the brand new one; the main stand was a bit tatty and with rust and what have you, there was a hole in the ground behind the other goal, and then you had the corrugated iron on the opposite side. There was only one place to take the pictures!

"It's a different club to what it is now, clearly. When you sit down with managers, they go through what's going to happen, and I sat down with Ken Bates as well. He showed me the model of Stamford Bridge and what it would be like. I have to say, I thought at the time that I didn't expect any of us would see that happening, but fair play – he got it built, he got it done. You've got to hope that what people are telling you is going to come to fruition. More often than not it doesn't, they just say what they think you want to hear."

For those readers who don't remember Hughes the footballer, the biggest compliment that can be paid to him is that he was a player hated by opposition supporters. His game was all about aggression, getting in the face of defenders and generally doing the dirty work to make life easier for his team-mates.

Only 12 months prior to joining the club he had scored in an FA Cup final against the Blues as Manchester United kept our trophy drought going by inflicting a 4-0 drubbing upon us at Wembley.

"Opposition fans didn't like me at all! That's just the way it was, that's the way I played. When I went to Chelsea, they were a little bit reluctant, initially, because I'd spent loads of years trying to be a pain in the backside to their club. I remember they'd cheer my name and then immediately start singing, 'We hate Man United' or 'Stand up if you hate Man U!'"

Soon, however, the supporters would grow to love him. In our FA Cup-winning season, they chose him as Chelsea's Player of the Year.

"I had a great time," Hughes says. "You could argue I had great times at United, won lots of trophies, but it was one of those things that the latter years were just about sustaining success, whereas the challenge for me was always, 'We've got to make a mark, we've got to start winning trophies again.' That's what happened at Chelsea and it's what I say to guys here when I'm trying to attract them to Stoke. I tell them, 'You can go to big clubs and be okay and win trophies and be in squads that win trophies, but really you're just sustaining success. You come, then you go, you're just sustaining the success the club's always had. Whereas if come to a club like this – or Chelsea as it was – and have success, people remember it.'"

And in 20 years' time someone will be interviewing you for a book about it.

"Exactly right! Someone will always buy you a free meal. I've been in football a long time and you make a few quid and whatever, but it's always nice to be remembered. That's about being able to make your mark and thankfully that team made its mark."

The prospect of making his mark at a club is something which crops up time and time again in our interview, which lasts just shy of an hour. That in itself is a minor miracle considering I was allocated half that time and we are twice interrupted by Stoke's chairman Peter Coates, who clearly has some pressing business to attend to with the manager.

In order to truly make your mark somewhere, you have to get up for the big occasions and deliver under immense pressure. It's clear that is something Hughes thrived upon, and at Chelsea there was added responsibility placed upon his broad shoulders.

"I always felt at Chelsea I had a different standing within the group than I had at United," Hughes says. "I'd been there for a long time and I was part of the furniture, really, but when I came to Chelsea it was like my standing in the group changed a little bit. I felt there was an onus on me, along with others, to really set the tone for what we were trying to do.

"I enjoyed it. I wasn't a tub thumper, screaming and shouting in the dressing room, I did it by example, just by virtue of how I approached the game and what I demanded from other people. It seemed to work for me."

Despite his role in the dressing room as one of the senior statesmen, many of Hughes's old colleagues were surprised he ended up becoming a manager.

"They wouldn't have seen that side of me," Hughes explains. "I was always an observer, someone who sat back and watched. I was a student of the game, I loved football; I loved watching games and trying to work out why something happened, why did a team concede there, how did they score that goal and so on. Towards the end of my career, which I clearly was reaching at Chelsea, I had changed and was thinking about the next step. I probably didn't know it at the time, but I was watching football more and enjoying it more by trying to work out what was going on. It was a different time in my career.

"I also played under three different managers there and learned from them all. Glenn had a really good understanding of the game. I'd been used to a different type of management, more autocratic. Fergie [Sir Alex Ferguson] didn't get involved in the training so much but he drove the training, if you know what I mean. It was delivered by somebody else but he was clearly the one in charge and dictated what we did, whereas Glenn was doing the sessions and imparting his knowledge as he went along. It was different for me, something I hadn't been exposed to, but I liked it for that reason.

"As for Ruud, his personality was very laid back, and he was there to enjoy life and to enjoy what he was doing. A completely different personality to the other managers. It's probably fair to say both him and Luca changed, to a certain extent, when they got the job. I always thought maybe that was a mistake in terms of how they went from being a player to a manager and changed their attitude towards players almost overnight, which confused people. I had a similar situation when I was a player with Wales and then I got the job as manager. I didn't say, 'Right, now you've got to call me boss,' or cut off any relationships I had formed with players when I was one of them. It was a more gradual thing, but by virtue of the job, distance forms anyway so you don't have to artificially create it overnight. It happens because your role changes, so you can't be as accessible. That's one thing I think both have them could have handled better. With hindsight, of course."

Another thing Hughes didn't take into his own managerial career was the example he set at Harlington, where he was the unanimous choice for the worst trainer award.

"Oh yeah," he says, grinning broadly. "I used to say, 'Monday, Tuesday, Wednesday – forget it.' The first two days I was getting the game from the weekend out of my system. And I always used to tell the lads I was practising, trying things in training that I wouldn't do in a game. More often than not they wouldn't come off, they'd be ridiculous things. I was hopeless Monday to Thursday, but Friday and Saturday I was great. And that was the most important thing. I used to pull their leg about that. If I was managing me I wouldn't be too happy about it! I cut them a little bit of slack now I'm a manager. I was never the greatest trainer in the world but I just used to get up for weekends really. That's what got me going."

Cup matches, in particular, seemed to bring the best out of him. His record in the FA Cup while at Chelsea was enviable: nine goals from 14 appearances. He netted twice in the 1997 semi-final win over Wimbledon and added further strikes in the last four of the League Cup and Cup Winners' Cup the following season, the latter a stunning half-volley, from his own headed flick-on, against Vicenza on an electric night at Stamford Bridge.

"Maybe my focus was a little bit better for those games," he says with a chuckle and a shake of the head. "League games are okay, but there's one after the other, and maybe my focus was better for one-off games. I always used to enjoy those. I used to sense atmospheres and I think that was part of maybe what supporters sensed from me. They could tell I would react to their reactions sometimes, and vice versa. That was part of how I got involved in the game. I think they sensed I knew how they were feeling. That's how it was at most clubs I was at.

"I'm a firm believer in the so-called 12th man, without a shadow of a doubt. I used it throughout my career to stimulate me to better performances. At times you had to try to make them understand that you maybe needed help and you had to engage with them and get them going. More often than not, Chelsea fans reacted to that."

If Hughes relied on the fans for help, he was the go-to-guy for his team-mates to lean on. In a spot of bother? Launch the ball up to Sparky. More often than not he would make it stick and bring others into play. In the years leading up to his move to Chelsea, he had acted as an on-field minder for Eric Cantona – indeed, he believes the Crystal Palace incident may never have occurred had he not been injured for the game.

When the Blues signed Gianluca Vialli in the summer of 1996, soon to be followed by Gianfranco Zola, Hughes was effectively employed as part strike partner, part bodyguard. The plan following Zola's arrival was to deploy the little maestro in the hole behind the two of them, and it certainly wasn't intended to bench a striker who had won the European Cup only a few months earlier. But it soon became clear the classic little and large strike pairing was the most effective selection.

"I think Luca struggled first year, in fairness, to get to grips with British football," Hughes recalls. "He'd come from Italy and part of his game was to go down a little bit too easily – and he would say that himself – and try to draw a foul and gain a free-kick. British referees weren't giving them. The summer after, he worked really hard on the physicality. He was a strong guy, but he just needed to resist challenges and understand that part of the game, and he worked really hard on that part of it and was better for it, so credit to him for that. But that was my game, really, resisting challenges, so I think that's why I got picked ahead of him.

"And Franco was just a joy to play with, one of the special players of that era. It was a good mix. I was just there to be a bit of a battering ram. He was an easy target because it was more aggressive in those days, refereed in a different way, and there was more leniency. You had the opportunity to stop good teams playing by being aggressive and that's what teams used to try and do. But he was a strong little guy, too. Deceptively so. He was always in the gym.

"I always say that smaller stature players have to be really exceptional to make an impact at the highest level, and that's why Franco was so good. He was able to affect almost every single game he played in. I played a part, maybe. I'd bash holes in the defence and he used to exploit that. But you've still got to be good enough to recognise situations if they present themselves. It was easy to play with Franco, easy."

Easier to play with than Cantona?

"They were similar. Eric and Gianfranco were constantly looking for areas where there was ittle pockets of space they could exploit and receive balls on the half-turn and drive. They were more difficult to pick up as a consequence; they'd come from deeper areas and arrive late, or look for one-v-one situations they could exploit. It was about understanding the game and recognising where they could hurt teams if they received the ball in certain areas. Very clever players and very different characters.

"Franco was more sociable, more gregarious around people, whereas Eric, believe it or not, has quite an introverted personality, completely different to the extrovert you saw on the pitch. Off it, he was quite quiet. He used to sit in the corner and observe and chuckle when he saw something funny. Zola was involved. He was just a nice guy and you enjoyed his company. They were different but equally effective as players.

"I was fortunate to play with great players throughout my career, some of the best to grace the Premier League and even before that, with Bryan Robson, Neville Southall, people like this. I was a decent player, but it's always easier when you surround yourself with great players and thankfully that's what I was able to do throughout my career."

With the chairman's latest visit indicating our time together has run its course, I have time for one last question. I choose to remind him of a comment he made in the aftermath of Chelsea's FA Cup win, when he spoke of the palpable sense of relief that could be felt around the club after lifting that first trophy and how breaking the cycle of failure is always the difficult part.

"I'd been through that at United and it was a catalyst for everything that followed," he reflects. "It's always there and you think, 'Come on, we need to get rid of this.' The league thing was massive at United. We'd won all the cup competitions

– the FA Cup, League Cup and Cup Winners' Cup – but the league was always the thing we were judged on. Prior to winning it, every year we didn't do it just made it harder and harder. To actually make it in the end was a huge thing. So, yeah, one of the main emotions was relief, and it was similar with Chelsea. I think it was a little bit different because I'd only been there a couple of years, but I could sense from the guys who had been there a long time, and people connected with the club a long time, there was a real relief and real pride that it was done.

"Once you do it [break the cycle], that group of players understands what it takes to win trophies. That's an important development for a group of players to understand, and to grow from that point onwards. I could see similar traits being displayed with this group that I saw with United. But clearly you need to keep bringing good players to the club, which obviously the club did from that point.

"It wasn't radical. The year I came there were two or three additions, then the same the next year and the year after that. Clearly the quality of player was of the required standard and standards were being raised right through the club. The attitude to what we were trying to do was different from when I first walked through the door to when I left three years after. We won three trophies in as many years and my only regret, personally, is that I didn't get on in the Cup Winners' Cup final. Apart from that I really enjoyed the three years there, which were comparable to the years I had at United in terms of enjoyment. It was a different sensation for me because I was viewed differently when I went to Chelsea and I really enjoyed that. And the club was in a different place when I left."

The sleeping giant had awoken.

4. Steady Eddie

'I've seen a heck of a lot and I've seen
the club go through some dramatic
changes: backwards, forwards, up
and down. There's not much that
can surprise me.'

Eddie Newton reaches across the table to pick up a photograph. A broad smile breaks out across his face.

"For me, what is most special about this is the person standing next to me."

In the picture, which was taken the day after the FA Cup final in 1997, he is stood alongside Frank Sinclair on the open-top bus which parades the players in front of thousands upon thousands of Blues supporters. Both of them have a hand on the trophy.

"We'd come through so much together," he explains. "I remember saying to him: 'Can you believe it, man? I met your scrawny backside on Barn Elms' pitch in a trial for west London schoolboys, thinking that was a massive thing to get into. And here we are, 12 years later, picking up the FA Cup.' We shared a lot of history together. It was fitting to stand next to him and hold the Cup together."

He tells me this in his office at the club's training ground, where he works as loan player technical coach. It is one of several positions he has had at a club he first joined in the mid-Eighties, and even our two-and-a-half-hour chat is barely enough to scratch the surface of his career with Chelsea.

He started here on a Youth Training Scheme (YTS) before graduating to the reserves and then, finally, the first team, where he was one of the few homegrown players to not only survive, but excel among the incoming foreign legion. Later on it was coaching. Assistant coach with the Under-10s, then manager. Under-11s head coach. Under-12s head coach. Under-16s assistant. Then away from the club as assistant to Roberto Di Matteo, his fellow FA Cup final scorer in 1997, with MK Dons and West Brom. Then assistant manager at Chelsea, winning the FA Cup and the Champions League.

Heading up the loans department. Caretaker manager, for one game, alongside Steve Holland. Assistant manager again. Now back to the loans.

"I've seen a heck of a lot and I've seen the club go through some dramatic changes: backwards, forwards, up and down. There's not much that can surprise me. I suppose the management roles are just like when I was a player – I played just about every position for Chelsea. You take things on board, take charge and do what you have to do. But nothing ever replaces being a footballer. Nothing. Every footballer will tell you that. It's a great feeling as a coach to win something, it's a close second best, but to be a player is such a different feeling. You're physically doing everything yourself, you're right in there. The adrenaline when you're playing is irreplaceable."

There are seemingly no grey areas as far as he is concerned. Whatever subject is thrown up during the course of our conversation, the one thing you can be sure of is that Newton will have an opinion on it and he will express himself with the same passion as a supporter but with the reasoned logic of someone who has been involved in the game for over 30 years.

"I am comfortable in my own skin and I'm not afraid to be myself," he says. "I will go my own way; not to go against the grain on purpose, just to be me. I won't go with the flow just because everyone's going with it. If it's not what I think is appropriate in the way I look at life then I won't go that way. I've been taught to be like that and it's naturally ingrained in me."

It was ever thus. Steve Clarke remembers the days when Newton and Sinclair were coming up through the youth set-up and banging on the door of the first team, and not one mention of their ability is made. If you've reached that stage, it's already apparent you're a good player, but it takes so much more than that to make it as a professional footballer. You need to have what football people describe as "that little something about you", which is on the borderline between confidence and arrogance channelled in the right way. There was no room for shrinking violets, least of all within the cut-throat nature of an early-Nineties dressing room, when tongues were sharper than any of the football played on the pitch.

"I remember one game when Steve was ripping into me and I snapped back at him," Newton recalls. "He put his arm around me and he liked the fact I'd snapped back at him. 'Listen,' he said. 'I only talk to you like that because I know you're a good player and in that situation you needed to do something better.' I really liked that. It was as we were coming off and it was a senior player taking on a senior role. Before we got to the dressing room he had calmed me down. I put my hand up and said I shouldn't have snapped back at him and I could see where he was coming from. And he said, 'It's no problem... but you need to see what I'm trying to tell you.' And I did. It was just that era, you could snap at someone. And you'd either take it or snap back. Then you'd deal with it and it was over. You go in the dressing room and get on with it."

Similar traits could be seen in John Terry when he came up to train with the first team as a 16-year-old. The story, which is now firmly ingrained in Chelsea folklore, is of JT going straight through the back of Dan Petrescu with a crunching challenge. The Romanian, as Clarke recalls, wanted "to fight JT, fight the world". Then, five minutes later, exactly the same scenario played out. Newton remembers it well.

"That was the way it was," he says. "Competitors were coming through, and it doesn't stop just because you get to train with the first team. 'No, mate – I want your position. I grew up at this club. This is my club.' That's how we used to think: This is my club. Don't come into this club and start telling me this or that. We would always look after our own. I remember telling Dan, 'Don't do that, mate.' We were very close as a squad, it didn't matter if you'd come from abroad or you'd come through at the club, but you just didn't mess around with one of the homegrown players. The motto of our youth team was: 'One in, all in.' If something happened on the pitch, everyone had to go in. No excuses. Everyone had to defend each other, help each other and fight for each other. Always, always, always. That's where that strong mentality came from, and we all had that coming through. It's something we're trying to develop with the youth players now and the players on loan. You're taking that final step into senior football, you have to have that will to fight."

There was no Academy at Chelsea back in the days when Newton was learning his trade, or indeed throughout his time as a player at the club. He describes a typical day as a YTS lad, which didn't actually involve an awful lot of training.

"You arrived at Stamford Bridge at 8 o'clock in the morning. You'd bag all the washing, all the kit, and then we'd drive over to Harlington, where you'd have to unpack the gear and put your player's kit, boots, towels and everything out. Our kit just got dumped in the middle of the room and you had to fight for it. It was a free-for-all, and you had to be strong to get the decent kit. Then, after training, you'd come in, do all your bits and pieces, bag the kit again and take it back to Stamford Bridge. You'd have to clean the stadium: the changing rooms, the upper tier, wherever. And you had to do some painting! It was a joke back then, but it made us what we were: a strong group. You got put through a lot but you stood up to it and you became a man very quickly.

"Although there was one time the coaches made the mistake of leaving us to it while we were supposed to clean the upper tier. Well, that was it. It was a hot day and the water fights got a little out of hand. We flooded the restaurants in the middle tier. Ken Bates was not a happy man! They got it in the ear, and that was it – they made us run for fun. We had some really great times. It was hard, really hard, but fun."

The story is relayed to me with a smile on his face throughout.

"I looked forward to going into training, to spending the day with my mates. It was a 12-hour day – you'd get in at 8am, leave at 8pm. We'd all have dinner together. There was a little kebab restaurant down the road and you had £2.50 to eat what you want. Everyone would end up in there and you'd eat kebab and chips, chicken and chips or whatever. Then you'd go home and that was your day."

His best mate was always Sinclair, who was a big part of the reason Newton joined Chelsea after pestering the coaching staff non-stop to bring him to the club while at the same time working at convincing his pal that a career with the Blues was worth pursuing instead of staying at Fulham. Eventually, persistence paid off and he made the switch to a club where he has spent, save for a few seasons here and there, the past three decades. So much has changed in that time, but not the lifelong bond he formed with Sinclair.

"I roomed with him for years and he gave me so much to laugh about," Newton says. "I can tell you many, many stories about Frank, but not for publication in this book! He's an extremely funny boy with a massive heart. You can't help but love the boy. Everything about him goes against the grain. His diet was a disgrace at times, but then he'd take his top off and he was ripped to bits. We'd be doing abdominal exercises and he'd basically do them completely wrong and not even get off the floor. 'How is your body like that? You're not even doing the exercise properly!' He'd just start laughing.

"But don't think he didn't work hard for it just because he was physically blessed. He's what, 5ft 9in or whatever, yet he could out-jump 6ft 2in players easily. His sprinting was incredible, good pace and good strength. And what I liked about Frank is that his self-confidence is unbelievable. He would always bet on himself to improve, and he improved technically every year. He got better and he made a fantastic career. I loved him on the football pitch because he's trustworthy, and that's something you always need. He'd give you everything, even if he was having a bad game. He'd try his best to do everything for the team."

Sinclair and Newton were the only two players from their age group in the youth team to make it through to the first team. Others, such as the goalkeeper Jason Winters and the striker Nathan Blake, went on to forge careers elsewhere at a lower level and there were other talented youngsters who fell by the wayside. The strong collective Newton talks about as a group did not materialise in terms of success at youth level.

"We should have done better," he admits. "I felt we had a group of players that should have gone on and won the league and gone into the latter stages of the FA Youth Cup. I don't think we took it as seriously. Our group of players were looking more towards senior football. I certainly did. I regret it now, we should have put more emphasis on the Youth Cup, but all I thought about was, 'I'm doing this to get where I really want to be, and that's first-team football.'

"In our day it was easier to get up there. But that's not to say it was easy. There was big competition and before you even think about playing against anyone else, you have to break down the competition in-house. That's a mindset I think we naturally had as a group when we were coming through the ranks. We were a very strong group mentally... a group of players that were hard to control. The coaches had to be right on top of us at all times. Believe me, they were.

"Apart from when Don Howe came in [under Ian Porterfield] I never really got coached again at the club until Glenn Hoddle was appointed. Most of the time you didn't really get coached."

Prior to Hoddle's arrival, Newton had played in numerous positions and never seemed to be given the chance to settle into a role. He made his debut as a left-back and showed signs of promise as a winger and even as a makeshift striker at White Hart Lane, when he scored twice to secure what was at the time a customary win at the home of Tottenham Hotspur. Now he was to be given a position to make his own, shielding the back four and, when in possession, to keep the ball moving quickly. He was to be the midfield metronome, more ticky-tocka than tiki-taka.

"I remember Glenn telling me, 'I've got a new position for you.' I was a bit worried when he started off with that line. Then he said it was as a holding midfielder. I looked at him. 'What's a holding midfielder?' We'd never played 3-5-2 before, but he wanted to bring a more continental way of playing to Chelsea. He said, 'I just want you to play in the holding role. I want to build the play through you, but also for you to be the first phase for the defence when we're getting attacked, to slow the opposition down and try to snuff out their attacks.'

"I was used to having big responsibilities from a young age.

My mum and dad had to work all the hours that God sent so I took on the job looking after my sister, who is nine years younger than me. I think I was quite a responsible young boy – I could cook and I could clean, so I took that kind of responsibility away from my parents. But at the same time I maintained playing football. Things were different back then, I don't think my parents could have got away with it now! But that's how it was. We got through and that's where I found my responsibility. I knew when to switch on and I could see I was a little bit different from some of my friends growing up. I had to mature very quickly as a young man and therefore it stood me in good stead for the future, particularly in this instance.

"It was very different to what I was used to playing in a 4-4-2, when we would share the responsibility of going forward and coming back. Now the offensive side, which I loved as well, was taken away from me, so I wasn't too happy about it. But that side of responsibility and the maturity to understand that you're giving something to the team, which is very important, came across and I took on the duty. I enjoyed it in the end."

When I ask him if he was the Claude Makelele of his time, only half joking, his response is deadly serious: "I was the first, without doubt. No one can deny that I was the first in that position to perform that role for Chelsea."

It is perhaps a step too far to say English football was stuck in a tactical rut of rigid 4-4-2 systems across the board, with little room for flexibility. The national team, for example, enjoyed its best run at a tournament since 1966 when they reached the semi-final of Italia '90 playing with three at the back, matching that performance at Euro '96 with a similar system, which came after manager Terry Venables had long flirted with a Christmas Tree formation. But it was not an exaggeration to say that straying from the norm with innovative tactics was undoubtedly viewed with suspicion.

"Back then they didn't understand it," Newton says. "Holding midfielder – what are you talking about? The No6 role – what's that? In England, the terminology didn't exist. I was the first and because I was the first, I didn't get the recognition. So be it. People began to analyse and understand Claude's role and what he used to do, and he did it extremely well. If Claude had been in my era, he'd have still been top at doing it but it would have gone over people's heads. Again, it's an era thing."

Recognition at the highest level so very nearly came his way, though. During Hoddle's third and final season at the helm, Newton was playing arguably his best football for the club and whispers of an international call-up were growing increasingly louder ahead of the European Championship to be held on these shores in the summer of 1996. Just as injury always seemed to hold him back at key moments earlier in his career, and would later bring a premature end to his playing days, he was handed a crushing blow in a game against West Ham.

"I was just really unlucky," Newton reflects. "I always got injured at the wrong time, it's the story of my career. Just as things started to get going. Venables was actually at that game to watch me, I was told that before we went out, and I was flying at the time, playing every game and in really good form. And then my lovely friend Kevin Hitchcock came flying out of the goal and broke my leg! I always remind him of it. Terry was looking at me to bring me in the squad, but that was that over and done with. I had another chance later on when Glenn was in charge, he wanted to bring to bring me to Le Tournoi, which was a little summer tournament in France the year before the World Cup. Glenn rang me up and I told him

I was going to have an operation on my knee after the 1997 Cup final. So that was gone again. Every time I was on the verge of international recognition I had an injury. It just wasn't meant to be."

Sinclair believes that, on his day, Newton was as good as Roy Keane and Paul Ince, widely viewed as the benchmark for combative midfielders in England in the mid-Nineties.

"I reckon I could mix it with them any day," Newton says. "I loved going up against them. It's competition and you can feel it as you're walking into the ground: 'This is going to be a hard game.' The levels you have to reach. Those are the games I loved. They used to go by so quickly, they'd just fly by, because your concentration levels, everything, was at the max.

"You can't hear the crowd, you're just so focused. You can ask strikers how they finished a goal and they can't tell you. I remember Rushy [Ian Rush], he'd be asked by the interviewer to talk them through the goal: 'I can't remember it.' You've just come off the field! But it's instinct, repetition of doing something over and over again, and the focus to make sure you do your job properly. That's what I suppose you call 'the zone'. That's the focus that drives you. Going up against the Man United boys, and later on Vieira and Petit, they were the matches you look for and really raise your game. We had great games against Man United and we really took it to them over the years, especially at Old Trafford. It was a challenge and I loved it. I always wanted a challenge."

In the 1994 FA Cup final, Newton conceded the penalty from which the Red Devils opened the scoring on their way to a 4-0 victory, and he would have loved the opportunity to make amends three years later.

"I remember after we beat Wimbledon in the 1997 semi-final

and everyone was going, 'Yeah, we could get Chesterfield in the final.' I'd have rather faced Man United again in the final, no hesitation. I'll tell you straight up, I would have been scared on the day, because of flashbacks to 1994 and all that, but yeah – the chance to redeem yourself properly. And if I'd scored in that game, oh my God, I'd have run into the crowd without doubt, I'd have jumped on someone's head! The game would have had to stop for my celebrations."

Instead, he had to settle for the consolation prize of scoring against *only* Middlesbrough. Aside from the obvious fact that we won the game, what was the biggest difference compared to how we approached the final in 1994?

"The biggest thing was inside the dressing room, where there was just a totally different focus," Newton remembers. "In 1994, all the talk beforehand was, 'You've got to enjoy the day. You never know if you're going to get back there again – go out and enjoy yourself.' Second time around, it was business. There was nothing said about enjoying the day or the occasion. That sort of thing is for the fans. It was a dressing room with a clear focus on winning the game, because that is all that mattered. You never know what's going to happen on the day, but there was far more confidence that we could go out and get the victory. For me to score, and right the wrongs of '94, was just the icing on the cake.

"I was blowing out of my backside just chasing after Robbie to celebrate his goal, so you can imagine how tired I was after 80-odd minutes. They had that Brazilian boy in midfield, I've forgotten his name. Emerson! That's it. What a strong boy. That was hard work. So, I was tired, but not gone. When Dan Petrescu overhit his cross, I saw Zola and I just knew he was going to do something so I carried on my run. He was our

Messi, he could score and create goals out of nothing and that's what made him different from anyone else. And he just popped it back into the area. It was perfect, straight onto my left foot. Glenn always used to say I had to stay behind the ball, and I was constantly behind the ball in that move!"

As with so many of his team-mates who played under Hoddle, Newton is glowing in his praise for the man who reignited his love of football. Watching that goal in the Cup final, his former gaffer would have been thrilled by the passing and movement on display; it was what he had attempted to bring to Chelsea coming to fruition on the grandest stage of all, four years in the making and requiring plenty of patience.

"We never went from back to front, we always played through the thirds," Newton says of the change in style under Hoddle. "We got hammered every home game by the crowd to begin with. They didn't understand it, they were so used to going from back to front. He's the one who talked to the fans through the programme notes, telling them the way we were going to play and why we were going to play like that. He educated the fans as we went along, until one day they started applauding the fact we strung 15 passes together and put a cross in and got a corner. They started clapping and we're looking around going, 'Wow, you're starting to get it.'"

The team's development continued at a pace when Gullit took over as manager.

"Under Ruud, one of your jobs as a player was to always be in a position to receive the ball. Always, always, always. We used to do so much work when it came to finding that position and being under pressure when receiving it, but also finding the solution. You should have one, two or maybe three options to find a solution to play out. That was a big part of

Ruudi's mantra. If we went into the wide areas, he used to hate someone getting to the byline and trying to whip a cross in under pressure and it gets knocked out for a corner. The crowd would all rise: 'Ahhhhh!' Just because we got a corner. He'd say, 'Why are you cheering just because we got a corner?' Instead, he wanted us to come out and we start again. We'll play out; come back to Eddie, then we'll switch the play and find another solution.

"Another thing Ruudi always used to say to us was to only cross if you're in a one-v-one situation and you've got the advantage in it. If they double up on you, don't try and cross. If we have to go all the way back, we'll do that and start again. That was his philosophy. The group dynamic bought into it and we tried to play that way. You can see by how we tried to construct our offensive actions."

The reaction to winning a corner remains exactly the same, though. The audible sighs can be heard when a player declines the opportunity to cross the ball and takes what, in the eyes of the supporters, is the safer route of playing the ball backwards.

"It will be in the English DNA for years. Still, when a long ball is headed down and someone scores, the fans go mad over it. Everyone says, 'Why don't we do that more often?' It's the English way. But lumping it long is a 50-50 at best. You're trying to take away the 50-50 and maintain the advantage. That's what we were doing."

The confidence of Gullit the footballer and then the manager had filtered down to the players. His man-management was criticised by those who didn't fit into the vision he had for Chelsea, but those who did had only positive things to say about his influence. Newton is one of them. He was recovering from the broken shin bone which had ended his season in the

February of 1996 and before the season was out he was paid a visit by the friend who would soon become his manager.

"Before Ruud had even taken the job, and when we didn't have a clue he was going to be offered it, I remember a conversation he had with me when I was still injured. 'Eddie, next season is an important one for you,' he said. 'We're going to do a lot through you. I can see a lot of football being played through you.' Okay. Who's been talking to him? I spoke to Michael Duberry and he'd had a similar conversation. 'You're better than what you are. Instead of coming through and heading the ball away like a typical English centre-back, I want you to bring the ball down.' He started talking to individuals, I could see it. Then he got the job and it all became clear. He started putting everything to plan.

"Early in the season I remember him saying he was two players short of competing with Man United for the league title. He put his fingers about an inch apart and said, 'We're that far away from winning the league. I believe this group of players should be competing for first or second.' One thing Ruudy was really, really good at was making you believe. He walked out the room. 'All right. Now we're going!' I loved it.

"He had a ruthless side, which was shown when he got rid of a few of the fans' favourites, but he knew his plan. Every successful manager has got a ruthless side, as does every successful footballer. To be at the top of the game, you have to have it. Everyone says Zola was a super gentleman – he was ruthless! He'd put you to the sword if he had to, but then he'd pick you up and say sorry and be a gentleman afterwards. You have to be ruthless. In life you have to make some hard decisions, and football is a career, it's business. You have to make hard decisions at vital times."

Everything was now centred on excellence, a far cry for what it had been like during Newton's early Chelsea career.

"There was no long-term strategy," he says. "Come in and train, no real direction, no real emphasis towards where we are going or what the plan is. There was none of it. We were just firefighting all the time, playing survival football. That's why I became disillusioned as a young guy. No disrespect to the players at that time or the coaches, I just think it was a culture that had developed in the club, even though they had been successful in the Seventies.

"That was another frustration of mine: all I ever heard about was the Seventies boys. And rightly so, because they were successful. We never should forget them, but surely we need to create something in the present and the future? But I couldn't see it, I just couldn't see it.

"Don't get me wrong, I've always loved being at this club, but I used to get really frustrated. I wanted to get the ball down and play, and people were panicking around me. This is not football. I want to win things and be part of something special. All my career, up to the first team at Chelsea, I played football. Always in footballing teams. In the youth team we always played football, never back to front. I went into the reserves with Mick McGiven and we always played football. Then you go to the first team and it's just – bang!

"I had to change my game for a while. You're watching it fly over your head and you need to anticipate where it's going to land. Then Glenn came and we were back to playing what I knew. I really, really started enjoying my football again and I was really proud of being at this club. We just went from strength to strength, we kept getting stronger and it didn't fade out. Everyone was going, 'Oh, they're just a cup team and this that and the other.' Then they started seeing us get stronger in the league and people started taking us seriously. You could tell. Man United, Liverpool and these boys were, by the way they were going at us, you could tell we were getting under their skin. And I loved that, I absolutely loved it."

Newton thrived in his midfield anchor role, although the arrival of a new defender from France required further adjustment.

"It was a bit frustrating for me when Frank Leboeuf came in, because before that I was used to everything going through me, and then all of a sudden he's going pew, pew, pew and pinging passes all over the place. And I'm like, 'Okay, that's enough!' But what a passer he was, which was something we hadn't really seen at Chelsea from a centre-half. We had to school him a little bit about English defending, though. I remember his first game against Wimbledon, when he ended up with a massive lump on his head. Afterwards he was complaining: 'This is not football.' I told him, 'This is England, mate.' It's not Europe, where someone blows on you and you get a free-kick. Doesn't happen here, anything goes and you get away with stupid tackles. Either learn quickly or you're going to suffer. And once everyone knows you can ping a ball 60 yards, they're not going to give you the room, they're going to rough you up, so get used to it. Quickly. And he did. He acclimatised, he realised he couldn't just do that all the time and he had to mix up his game."

The influx of quality players changed not only the dressing room but the whole culture of the club. After a training session, instead of going home, the players would now stay behind to do extra work.

"Everyone was doing personal drills – free-kicks, strikers

doing finishing with a coach, midfielders doing passing drills or working on your first touch under pressure, things like that. All of a sudden, the focus had changed. It's how it should be, looking towards achieving better and better things. It wasn't just about reaching cup finals – it was winning them. Once you start winning cup finals, you start looking towards the league and Europe. All of a sudden it's a different ball game."

The club has never looked back. By the time Newton was part of the first-team coaching set up, the wait wasn't for any major trophy, it was *the* major trophy they were pining for – the Champions League. He remembers sitting in the dressing room at the Allianz Arena after the greatest moment in Chelsea's history.

"It was just a picture looking at all their faces," Newton recalls. "I remember giving Florent Malouda a hug and then afterwards he was just looking into the abyss. His face said it all: 'I've finally done it. I can't believe we've finally done it.' The club had been chasing this for a long time."

The days of supporters having to hark back to the glory days of the Seventies are long gone, just as 1997 is now remembered as the stepping stone to bigger and better things. The players who helped put Chelsea Football Club on the path to success will never be forgotten and deserve to be celebrated, but as Newton says, it's all about creating something special in the present and the future. Writing history, not only reliving it.

FRANK SINCLAIR

5. Fun Time Frankie

'I'd pictured it for so many years and put on a Chelsea shirt so many times since I was a kid, but this was *the* Chelsea shirt. Not the youths, not the reserves - the first team. I had pictured the moment in my mind and dreamed about it all the time.'

Frank Sinclair entered the dressing room and began sorting through the mess. Champagne bottles were everywhere, the corks popped in celebration littering the floor, and the players were a long way from being finished. Judging by the celebrations, it was hard to tell if it was the first trophy they'd ever won, but the moment was going to be cherished as if it was the last. You never want to lose that winning feeling.

"Kenny Dalglish had scored the winner. I was a ballboy behind the goal at the end he volleyed the ball home, a goal which meant Liverpool won the league at Stamford Bridge. My second duty that day was to clean the away dressing room, and I can tell you now that place was a mess! The Liverpool players were still in their kit because they'd been celebrating for so long and I remember just sitting there and staring at Kenny. What a player he was. He was swigging away at his champagne and I had to snap out of it and start cleaning up after him. Some teams wouldn't allow you in early, which was annoying because you just wanted to get the job done as quickly as possible so you could go home, but Liverpool let us in that day and it was incredible to look around the dressing room and rub shoulders with all those top players. I just kept my head down and did my job.

"Chelsea at the time was not an elite club, we were middle of the road, and you didn't see that sort of thing happening in our dressing room."

That was in 1986, when Sinclair was a 14-year-old boy still trying to make his way in the game. Fast forward 30 years and he has only just come to the end of a career which saw him win three major honours with his boyhood club followed by a League Cup at Leicester City, represent Jamaica at a World Cup and appear at every single level of the Football League

– and even a couple of tiers below – as he extended his playing days into his mid-forties. From playing in front of tens of thousands of spectators to a couple of hundred. All for the love of the game.

His biggest passion will always be Chelsea, though, and he still pulls on the famous blue shirt on a regular basis at Stamford Bridge, albeit confined to the studio of Chelsea TV as one of its pundits for the *Wherever They May Be* show which is filmed for every away game.

It was 26 years ago that he donned the Blues kit for his first-team debut under very different circumstances. Bobby Campbell was the Chelsea manager and the club was toddling along in mid-table with a side packed full of homegrown talents when he decided to give the latest youngster off the conveyor belt his big opportunity for a match at home to Luton Town towards the end of another uneventful season. There was nothing at stake for either side, but for Sinclair it was a moment that was eight years in the making.

"I'd geared myself up for it since the very first day I joined the football club at the age of 11," he says. "I had pictured the moment in my mind and dreamed about it all the time. That was my main focus. When it finally happened, as incredible it was, the overriding emotion was relief. I'd pictured it for so many years and put on a Chelsea shirt so many times since I was a kid, but this was *the* Chelsea shirt. Not the youths, not the reserves, the first team, in front of 28,000 fans or whatever it was. I'm here now. This is the time to show what I'm made of."

Perhaps it felt like 28,000 to a 19-year-old making his professional bow, but the official attendance figure was closer to the 12,000 mark, which was the lowest home gate of the season and way below the average of 20,000. The stayaways missed out on perhaps the most thrilling match of the campaign.

"There were a lot of different emotions that day, let me tell you, and plenty during the week, too," Sinclair recalls. "Bobby pulled me and Eddie [Newton] to let us know we were going to make our debuts, but on one condition. We both had quite long, curly hair on top, as was the fashion at the time, but it'd have to come off if we were going to make our debut. Eddie got injured – story of his life, especially as a young pro, which held him back and was a test of character – and he didn't have to cut his hair.

"There were a lot of nerves in the build-up to the game, but it really reassured me to have a lot of players in that side who I had grown up with. It must have been Chelsea's youngest-ever back four: there was me, a 19-year-old, at left-back; the two centre-halves were David Lee and Jason Cundy, who were both 21; and then you had Gareth Hall, 22, at right-back.

"For all the nerves in the build-up, I knew I trained with the players all the time and I felt part of it. I felt good enough in training and I had a lot of self belief going into the game. Then we went 3-0 down within about 20 minutes! I thought it was a disaster, it couldn't have gone any worse. At half-time I was doubting myself. Was I the reason things had gone so badly? I picked myself up and I actually had a decent game. Incredibly, with 10 men we came back and drew 3-3. What a comeback. It was a game with so many emotions and I will never forget it."

Even today he wears the shirt well and it's not difficult to see how he managed to prolong his playing career until midway through his fifth decade, although it's harder to believe when you've listened to his good mate Eddie Newton harangue him for his slipshod approach to fitness training and his shocking diet. Indeed, the first time I ever met Sinclair was as a 10-year-old boy in the Walton-upon-Thames branch of McDonald's, where he was tucking into his breakfast the day after a game.

Today, he declines the bowl of nuts which has been placed at our table at the Copthorne Hotel at Stamford Bridge and also turns down my offer of a pint, preferring instead to order a glass of rosé wine with "lots of lemonade". Although no longer playing, he still keeps fit by boxing, a big passion for a man whose middle name is Muhammad thanks to his father's love of the most iconic boxer of all time. His older brother, Ian, took it one step further, boxing for his country for many years.

Sinclair was also a regular at Fitzroy Lodge, the gym where Ian trained, and had even begun sparring himself as a nine-year-old. Then his life changed forever.

"I went to Stamford Bridge for my first game around the same time as I started boxing," he recalls. "It was a class trip when I was at Pimlico School and I was fortunate enough to be one of maybe 15 kids to go. I'd always followed Liverpool because that was the team my brother supported, but as soon as I went to my first game that changed. I honestly couldn't tell you who Chelsea were playing against, I just remember the passion of the supporters and I fell in love with the club straight away, I was hooked. And I got a lot of stick from my brother because of it! I knew I wanted to become a footballer. Besides, in sparring I got punched on the nose a few times and those eye-watering shots didn't really appeal to me that much!

"Growing up in Clapham, it was quite a rough area at the time and I was brought up on a council estate, so it would have been easy to be misled by people. But I was so dedicated to what I wanted. I was raised by my mum and she's very religious. I think she wanted me to be more of a churchgoer, but I could never go because I always played on a Sunday. But she understood. A big thing for my mum and why she supported me was because football was keeping me out of trouble."

Once he was invited to train at Chelsea as an 11-year-old, you couldn't keep him away from Stamford Bridge.

"I came to every single home game after I joined the club. Schoolboy footballers had the chance to be a ballboy at matches, so I was regularly at Stamford Bridge, taking it all in. I used to ballboy for the reserves as well, so I spent a lot of my youth growing into a teenager at the football club. I just felt so much a part of it. I used to come in from the age of 14 and 15 and train with the youth team. I'd get days off school to come in and train, it was brilliant. I think they classed it as work experience and they explained it to my school that it was simply preparing me to be a professional footballer. And it was – 30 years later I was still playing!"

He recalls a story from around that time when he met the DJ and lifelong Chelsea fan Trevor Nelson, when they were both young hopefuls with big dreams for the future.

"We were in a kitchen at a house party in Clapham and he had not yet made a name for himself," Sinclair explains. "We started talking. There was me, him and another girl, and we were all saying what we wanted to be. I hadn't cracked it at Chelsea, I was still playing in the reserves, so I said I wanted to be a professional footballer; Trevor said he wanted to be a DJ; and the girl, whose name is Sarah, said she wanted to be a singer. Obviously I ended up playing for Chelsea, Trevor became a huge DJ and Sarah ended up joining a famous group called *Arrested Development.* Well, I'm pretty sure that was their name anyway! We all achieved our goals and it's something I've never forgotten."

Confidence has never been an issue for Sinclair, and it still isn't to this day. While discussing a recent spell working with Stoke City's Under-23s, he informs me he'd join in training on a regular basis and was "still the best player, whatever anyone else says". A smile accompanies this statement.

"I was always was a confident lad," he says. "I remember the first day I came to the club as an 11-year-old. I came straight from school and went to the old offices with all the ivy on them. I was shown around the stadium and when we went into the changing rooms there was a player sat down. 'Do you know who that is?' And I said, 'Yeah, it's Joey Jones. Top player, left-back.'

"He started talking to me, asking me a load of questions, and I couldn't believe I was having this conversation with one of my heroes. I asked him, 'What number do you wear.' He said, 'No3.' 'And what peg number are you in the bootroom?' No3 again. I said, 'When I make it, I'm going to wear No3 and have the No3 peg.' The day I signed professional forms I walked into the bootroom and No3 was clear. I was buzzing! And whatever position I played, for many years I wore the No3 shirt, even if I wasn't play left-back."

Once a youngster is integrated into the first-team set-up, it is critical there are players within the squad who are able to set the right example and help a young player along with a guiding hand. As Sinclair has already alluded to, there were not many senior players in defensive positions, but that was about to change with the purchase of Paul Elliott from Celtic.

"As a player, he was the biggest role model I had in the game," he says. "He took a lot of time to help me out, both on and off the pitch. We actually travelled in together quite regularly. I'd pick him up from the train station and drive him into Harlington, so we spent a lot of time in the car together. You could tell he was well educated by the way he spoke and how he carried himself. I just admired him so much as a person. And as a player he was fantastic, in my opinion one of the best not to play for England. One of my big regrets was not getting the opportunity to play and learn my trade out there on the pitch alongside him.

"He suffered a career-ending injury at Liverpool early into his second season and that's what gave me the opportunity to get into the team. I ended up Player of the Year! I'd been thrown in at the deep end, sink or swim really, and being a new kid on the block, the supporters took to me massively. I felt at ease and was really confident that season, but what people didn't see was that behind the scenes Paul was helping me massively, even while he was trying to come back from a horrible injury.

"If people ask me my regrets in the game, the big one was not being able to play and learn from him on the pitch. No disrespect to David Lee, Erland Johnsen, Jakob Kjeldbjerg, Mal Donaghy and people like that, but I felt I was at a level where I didn't really learn that much off of them as players. I just learned from playing games, getting the experience that comes with that. If I'd played with Paul, I think it maybe would have elevated me a level. Maybe I'd have played for England."

The biggest lesson was instead lurking just around the corner. The season after winning Player of the Year, Sinclair was a regular fixture in the side which led Chelsea to a first FA Cup final in 24 years. Although the Blues were underdogs against Manchester United, there was cause for optimism that an upset was on the cards after we had beaten the newly crowned Premier League champions home and away, both matches settled 1-0 in our favour by a Gavin Peacock goal.

On a miserable day at Wembley, the kind which is rarely to be found on FA Cup final day, the Blues were blown away after edging a goalless second half, losing 4-0. Newton had conceded the penalty from which United opened the scoring and they were given another chance to double their lead from the spot when Sinclair was wrongly adjudged to have fouled Andrei Kanchelskis. A third followed soon after when the visibly upset youngster slipped to allow Mark Hughes a chance which he wasn't about to pass up. The camera panned to Sinclair as tears streamed down his cheeks.

"I lost my composure and the penalty decision threw me," he reflects. "Eddie's was a stonewall penalty, so he could roll his sleeves up and get on with the match, but I couldn't accept the ref had given one against me. I was definitely still thinking about the decision when I gave the third goal away, still upset.

"The biggest thing I learned that day was how to react after a negative. We were playing so well and we should have gone in 1-0 up – only inches away from Gavin Peacock's volley going in instead of hitting the bar. We were so confident going into the second half and I don't think we really thought about Man United not being able to play that badly again in the second half.

"When we conceded, we just went all out attack to get back at them. There was no composure. It wasn't just me, it went through the whole team. If we'd taken our time, given us 15 or 20 minutes to get back into it, it was only one goal. But we went straight at them, leaving ourselves short at the back, and ended up conceding four goals. That was the biggest learning curve for me.

"After the game, I think Eddie actually took it a bit harder than me because it was the first penalty and it changed the game totally. Also, I think I had thicker skin than him. I'd had a lot of knock-backs throughout my career and just dealt with it. On to the next hurdle. But Eddie said something to me in the changing room which we both remember to this day: 'That isn't the end of it. I'm coming back and putting it right.' I believed him and he made me believe. We were always so competitive the two of us, going right back to when we were kids. We both thought we were the best two players. Every time he got better, I felt I had to get better. It really helped bring us both on. And I felt the same at that moment. I just thought, 'Well, if Eddie's going to do something about this, I've got to as well!'"

In years gone by, such an opportunity wouldn't have come his way again, at least not at Chelsea. But the good times were on their way back. We may have looked out of place on that first trip to Wembley, but it was the first step on the path to greatness, one which was improved upon year after year from here on in. The return to European competition in the Cup Winners' Cup brought about increased professionalism in terms of preparation for matches and it was impossible not to be caught up in the excitement of that.

"The atmosphere at the European games was unbelievable and you could feel the buzz immediately," Sinclair recalls. "With me being a fairly local London lad, I'd drive in and as soon as you got anywhere near Chelsea – even out Hammersmith way

– you'd see blue shirts making their way to the ground. It used to give me an unbelievable buzz.

"There was always something special about playing at Stamford Bridge at night. The biggest games I remember were the European nights, along with the Liverpool comeback in the FA Cup. There was just a special atmosphere, you could feel it in the air.

"We were so well prepared for every opponent, and for that you've got to give Glenn Hoddle credit. He did his homework on the opposition and it was detailed analysis on what to expect from everyone. We worked on it a hell of a lot in training and there were no surprises for us throughout that run. We knew who we were coming up against, what their strengths were, where their weaknesses were. I'd give Glenn a lot of credit for us getting us to the semi-finals. It was our first time in Europe for decades and we weren't a massive team so I think people underestimated us. Once we'd had that taste, we wanted more."

Sinclair had to wait another couple of years before experiencing European football again, by which point the squad had undergone a significant overhaul, and the arrival of one player in particular had a big influence on his own game.

"We had all of these new stars coming into the club and it was a brilliant experience for me being a youngster at the time as it gave me the opportunity to learn from some outstanding professionals," he says. "It definitely made me a better player, just watching the way they were working in training and the dedication to improvement. Gianfranco Zola was brilliant at free-kicks, but he'd still be out there practising with 50 balls – 25 of them would fly into the top corner, but then he'd still do another 25. It was unbelievable to see the dedication of the foreigners that came over at the time, what they brought to the sport.

"I was never surprised by what Gianfranco did on a football pitch because I saw it in training week in, week out. He was the first person to carry the balls out on the training pitch and the last to leave. I did a lot of individual work with him because he used to like doing one-v-ones with me so we'd stay out with a bag of balls, sometimes with Kevin Hitchcock, and I'd be defending against one of the most talented players who has ever played in the Premier League.

"He had a turn of pace and the ability to change direction at ease, but I was quick and I could recover, so that's why he used to like doing it against me. Little did I know at the time that he was improving me as a player at the same time because if I could cope with Gianfranco Zola on a regular basis then there's not many other players who can give me problems like that. The thing is, he never stopped to give me pointers – he would just torture me!

"I was learning on the job and he would try and twist me into the ground and score as many goals as he could. Me being a proud person, I didn't make it easy for him. He got the odd kick every now and then, but I always made sure it was never too hard because I wanted him fit for the Saturday."

Redemption came his way at Wembley in 1997, the icing on the cake delivered by the left boot of his good friend Newton to bring the FA Cup back to west London.

"Obviously, I was happy he killed the game off, I was buzzing for him, but at the same time I was gutted. Knowing Eddie like I did from the age of 11, I was never going to hear the last of it! The other thing was that he saved himself £50. Every year we used to have a little bet between us about who would score the most goals. It was free money for Eddie because he often played attacking midfield, sometimes even up front. And I was ahead of him by one that season until he scored that goal..."

A year later we were back for the Coca-Cola Cup final at the same venue and against the same opposition. This time there was no early goal to settle us down, and the scoreboard at full-time remained as it did at kick-off. Extra time beckoned.

"I'd given everything I thought I had to give in normal time," Sinclair says. "I was knackered. Suddenly, Luca took off Dan Petrescu and moved me to right wing-back. What is he doing? Dan was probably the best wing-back in the world, certainly in the top three. All I could think was, 'How am I going to get through extra time?'

"Paul Gascoigne played a loose pass and I picked the ball up in the middle of the park and played it on to Zola. I was on auto-pilot, I just kept going. Zola slotted in Dennis Wise out wide and as I started running into the box, I had a vision of what Wisey was going to do. I'd seen him do it in training so many times – if he was struggling to get to a ball, he'd cross the ball as he fell over. I saw his loose touch, and Wisey wasn't the quickest, so I knew what was coming and I pictured it in my head. So I was prepared for it, probably the only one in the box anticipating it, and he put it on a plate for me. A lot of my goals were headers, I could get a lot of power behind the ball and I had a good leap considering I'm only 5ft 9in. I met the ball at its highest point and headed it down. I couldn't get power on it because of how it was floated in, so I just had to make it awkward for the keeper.

"When it hit the back of the net, I knew I had to celebrate, you get that tingle in your stomach when you score a goal which I can't really describe, but I was too tired. I ran for a little bit and then just collapsed. The first thing that popped into my head is that I couldn't wait to speak to Eddie and tell him I'd scored at Wembley. I was just on the ground shouting, 'I can't believe I've scored' and all I remember was Gianfranco Zola jumping on top of me shouting, 'Believe it! Believe it!'"

Sinclair had been carrying an injury during the latter stages of the match. Little did he know it would be his last game as a Chelsea player.

"I scored that goal with a groin strain and I don't think we had another sub, so I carried on, which obviously made it worse. There was no way I was coming off and leaving us down to 10 men. But I knew I was doing more and more damage as the game went on and I knew the Cup Winners' Cup semi-final was on the way. I got through it, but I had a fully blown groin strain.

"There's definitely mixed feelings whenever I see that goal. It was the most important one of my career, on such a big occasion, but as proud as I am to have done it in my last game, there's the disappointment of it being the last time I ever pulled on the Chelsea shirt.

"Realistically, Gianluca Vialli didn't want me to go but Ken Bates did. We'd just signed Marcel Desailly and Albert Ferrer and I knew my opportunities would dwindle and I had a big think. Did I want to stay at the club and have a bit-part role, even though we were on the way up? Would I enjoy that? Or did I want to carry on playing regularly? I was only 26 and I just thought I had so much more football in front of me. I was just about to go to the World Cup as well. I had to leave, but it was one of the hardest decisions of my life."

To the surprise of every one of his team-mates, Sinclair was the last of the 1996/97 side to hang up his boots, finally calling it quits in 2015 at the age of 43. Even then it wasn't an easy decision.

"It's not that I was finding it difficult, but as you get older you realise you're having less and less of an effect on the game," he explains. "Throughout my career, one thing I prided myself on was being able to affect games at every level I played, and that was mainly the reason why I dropped down the levels. I went from the Premier League right the way down the ladder and at every level I still thought, even though I was getting older, ability-wise I could affect the success of the teams I was playing for.

"I still felt fit enough and good enough to play, but I also enjoyed the development side. I remember helping Gary Cahill when he was taking his first steps as a professional on loan at Burnley, and all through my career I played with centre-halves who were younger than me and I had the chance to aid their development when I played with them. That kept me young as a player. That added responsibility I put on my shoulders was something I used to keep me going and to keep the fire in my belly to continue playing.

"I'd have loved to have seen out my career in the Premier League, and especially at Chelsea, but you're at the end of the phone, waiting for it to ring and an opportunity to play."

FRANK LEBOEUF

6. Role Player

'In England, football is a religion.
When you play at Wembley or any
stadium, you can feel the passion.
It's amazing. The atmosphere is
really special.'

"I've dreamed of this since I was a little boy."

How often have you heard that line uttered by professional footballers? They dream of playing at Wembley; winning a major cup final; pulling on the shirt of a particular team or representing their country.

Frank Leboeuf was different. Of course he was. Growing up in Bouches-du-Rhone, a small village which is located between Marseille and Toulon on the French Riviera – "A very nice climate," he informs me on a freezing December morning in London two days before Christmas – as the middle child of three boys, Leboeuf had an altogether different vision for his future.

"When I was four years old, I wanted to be an actor," is a revelation that will not come as a shock to anyone who had the privilege of watching a player with greater technical abilities than perhaps any other centre-half to kick a ball for Chelsea Football Club, but one whose penchant for the amateur dramatics could amuse and infuriate in equal measures.

"But, for me, acting or playing in theatre was in Paris, so it was probably quite impossible to reach it. My father trained with the little academy in my village and I only played football for fun. It was only when I was 13 or 14 I realised it could be a business."

Perhaps it was impossible for the young Frank to live out his dream, but he is making up for lost time now. Shortly after our interview, he is set to embark on a four-month run of the play *Ma Belle-mere Et Moi Neuf Mois Apres* [My Mother-in-law And Me Nine Months After], which he co-wrote, co-directed and stars in. It is the follow up to *Ma Melle-mere, Mon Ex Et Moi* [My Mother-in-law, My Ex And Me]. Both are comedies.

"Then we're going to go on a tour of France, Belgium,

Switzerland and Luxembourg," he informs me. "A European campaign, if you like, for French-speaking people. It's the second play we have done, a friend and I. For the last two years we played 650 times in Paris and on tour. It's a good achievement for us. I came back to my first passion, which was movies and plays as well.

"I actually started my acting career at Chelsea. I met Ronnie Harwood, who wrote *Taking Sides* as a play, and it was shown in France many times, and I shared with him my passion for acting. Two years later, he called me and said, '*Taking Sides* is becoming a movie and I want you to be in it.' I was pretty sure it was kind of a joke, that it wasn't true. Even when I was in the make-up room before shooting, I was with Harvey Keitel, and he was asking me in which movies had I appeared before. 'None. I'm not even an actor!' And he said, 'What the eff are you doing here!' I just said, 'I don't even know, man.' It was the first steps in a new career."

And what a journey it's been.

"I was told that I'm the first football player in the world to win the World Cup and be in an Oscar-nominated movie," he says of his cameo as a doctor in the Stephen Hawking biopic *The Theory of Everything*, which set tongues wagging among football supporters in this country, many of whom will have heard little about Leboeuf since his departure from these shores in 2001.

"If we'd won the Oscar for the Best Movie I would have had the statue as well, so I would have been able to put it with the World Cup and the other medals. But I have to thank Chelsea for that, it's why I'm a big fan. Sometimes during the Champions League, when Chelsea played, for example, Paris Saint-Germain, people asked me who is my favourite and I'd reply, 'I cannot say Paris because I have to be fair to Chelsea. I have to be faithful to Chelsea.' The club brought something special for me. I won all of my trophies during my time there, including with the national team. Chelsea is my club and it will be forever."

Listening to Leboeuf speak passionately about his gratitude for the club which put him on the footballing map takes me back to his arrival on these shores in 1996. Chelsea fans had no idea who he was. Had you shown me a picture of this slim, balding centre-half without any information, I'd have probably guessed he was a player from the Seventies; he just had the look of a footballer from a bygone era. Then we saw him play. Wow!

Chelsea's long, drawn-out affair with the sweeper position began with Tommy Docherty in the Sixties, who deployed Marvin Hinton in the role during our run to the Fairs Cup semi-final, and came back with a vengeance in the Nineties, but only after Graham Roberts' brief but spectacular dalliance with it.

It is not often that we looked across west London for the blueprint, but in Queens Park Rangers we had the perfect example of how to make three at the back a success. In 1987, Jim Smith introduced that tactic at Loftus Road, utilising the man-marking skills of Paul Parker and Alan McDonald either side of the sweeper, Terry Fenwick. Smith's assistant at QPR was none other than Peter Shreeves, who went on to work alongside Glenn Hoddle at Chelsea when the manager decided to play himself as the sweeper in a three-man defence. It quickly became apparent he was thinking two or three steps ahead of his team-mates, many of whom freely admitted their manager was the most talented player in the squad, and it was far from a successful tactical switch. It was a similar story with Ruud Gullit when he arrived in 1995, ending up with the Dutchman moving into midfield. Neither of them were natural defenders, but the same could not be said of Leboeuf who, we would soon discover, beneath the silky exterior possessed a steeliness which let opposition centre-forwards know he meant business.

"Have we got a world-class defender in this country?" asked the club's matchday programme at the start of the 1996/97 season. "Why did we go to France to buy Frank Leboeuf? He's got pace, he's strong, determined, he reads situations, intercepts a lot of balls. He's brave, good in the air. What a boy! And he can play when he's got the ball. Questions are now being asked about the art of defending, and that's a good thing. Not only the art of defending, but can they control a ball, show skills. Not just defend but play their way out of trouble. At Chelsea we teach good habits from an early age. Hopefully in the near future we'll be producing defenders who can play, and play not only for Chelsea but for their country as well."

Those questions were answered emphatically by John Terry a few years later, but in Leboeuf we had a pioneer in the art of mixing the skill set of a midfield player and a traditional centre-half. On his debut against Southampton at the Dell, fans were dumbfounded by the manner in which their new defender sprayed the ball around the pitch, as if he had the football on a string. The confidence with which he strode out of defence, in or out of possession, gave credence to Gullit's sexy football mantra.

When the Dutchman came out with those immortal words, it is unlikely Erland Johnsen crossing for fellow centre-back Leboeuf to open the scoring against a garishly attired Coventry

City side early in the season was quite what he had in mind. It certainly wasn't Total Football at its finest, but that passage of play, in its own little way, illustrated the change that was starting to occur in west London. The opening goal against the Sky Blues displayed the freedom and fluency which Gullit wanted to see from his Chelsea side, with Leboeuf at the forefront of that. Our French revolutionary.

Leboeuf soon became known for his goalscoring as much as his defending, thanks to his deadly penalty-taking as well as his eye for an inch-perfect long ball over the opposition defence, not to mention a penchant for a laser-guided thunderbolt from distance.

"I was a defender who had previously played midfield, even when I was a professional," he says. "So for me it wasn't only about taking the ball and playing kick and rush, it was about playing the ball to my midfield and my strikers. The type of football Ruud wanted to see on the pitch was exactly the way I wanted to play – with attacking thoughts and also freedom for everybody. When you go to Italy, most defenders are not allowed to cross the middle line on the field. That wasn't my football.

"I was actually criticised by other sweepers and defenders! But it's why Ruud signed me, because he wanted to play football from the back and he thought I was the right guy for that. It worked very well at the beginning."

Although it was sometimes lost among his eye-catching work in the offensive half, he brought a calm assuredness and reading of the game to our defence and it was not by coincidence that each of the finals won during his five seasons at the Bridge were accompanied by clean sheets. Any chinks which appeared in his armour – his hot-headedness was perhaps on display too

114

often – were comfortably outweighed by the positives.

Had he been frozen in 1996 and thawed out today, how much would he be worth? He lets out an audible gasp and then pauses for dramatic effect; the years spent in LA learning the acting trade come to the fore.

"I don't know. We talked recently on our radio show about the salaries of players – and someone who had signed for PSG for maybe €8 million, tax free, per year – and I was just, 'Wow. Wow. Wow.' I was so far away from there when I was playing for Chelsea. It's funny that I was signed for something like £2 million, £2.5 million, which is nothing now. Di Matteo was £4.9 million or something like that. So, I don't know what I would be worth, you have to tell me."

I suggest a starting figure of £50 million.

"Well at the time I was completely unknown, nobody knew me. I wasn't even known in France, it was only after the World Cup final in '98 that people there realised that maybe I was a good player. Playing for Chelsea made me known in other parts of the world because the Premier League is watched everywhere. So, at that time, I guess it wouldn't be that much."

Then let's fast-forward a year to 1997, after a stunning first season in England.

"Oh yeah, maybe that amount," he says, although I suspect there is a hint of sarcasm in his answer. "I don't know, it's hard to say really. I don't think anyone is worth that money, it's just an offer and demands and how the market works. Is there a price for a human? It's in slavery that we have the price for a man and a woman. But football is a business, so it depends on many, many things."

In a football landscape where bland soundbites dominate, it's lamentable that a player such as Leboeuf would be unable to speak as freely were he playing today for fear of the repercussions. His public put-downs of David Beckham and Dennis Bergkamp, in particular, were scathing. He described the Dutchman as "a very good player but a s**t man," after one match against a striker who, for all his grace, was never afraid to lead with an elbow or leave his foot in. He insists the comments were not meant to cause a stir or to make the headlines, but to inform football fans that perhaps they were worshipping false idols.

"Sometimes I went maybe too far, because there's no doubt Bergkamp was a fantastic player, but sometimes behind the fantastic player you see stuff, because you're alongside them, that people don't see. I don't want to go back and I hope I didn't hurt him too much, but sometimes you are hurt on the field because a guy stamps on your toes or whatever and you react by saying stuff.

"But it's like I said to David Beckham when I saw him in Los Angeles: 'We had some bad times together, but the career is over, I'm another person and I hope when we see each other we're gonna have a good time!' Now I'm not as touchy as I was before! At the time, people asked me about them and I only said the truth. It was a little bit too much, maybe. I'm a Buddhist now so I wouldn't have said it like that."

Leboeuf's spiritual awakening followed a difficult period in his personal life. Within four months of hanging up his boots in 2005, he had lost his father and got divorced.

"It was a little too much for one guy... and so I struggled for like two years," he reveals. "I had a chance to see a lecture from the Dalai Lama and he was saying some stuff that was interesting – it's not, for me, a religion, it's a philosophy.

"Something touched me when he said, 'People ask me what

do you think about this, what do you think about that? And I tell them I don't know anything. It's just human to say to the others that I don't know. It doesn't make you stupid, it makes you interested of learning.' I thought to myself, 'That's a good point, this guy is clever.' I wake up every morning saying, 'I will try to be happy today and I will try to not bother anybody.' I think if everybody was thinking the same you wouldn't see any war, you wouldn't see any terrorist attack, anything. Just people trying to be happy. That's it."

It's also why he is now able to shrug off his infamous appearance on *They Think It's All Over*, the BBC's satirical sports-based panel show, aired exactly four months after he had become a world champion, when he humorously gave the same answer to every question: "I don't care – I won the World Cup." It became a stick with which Leboeuf has been repeatedly beaten over the years, and on a later edition of the show they claimed he had even blamed his rough treatment at the hands of opposition strikers on his appearance. Although as host Nick Hancock pointed out, "How thick would a Premier League footballer have to be to take Frank's remarks on this show seriously?"

"It was just a joke," he reiterates. There is a hint of exasperation in his voice; is this really what I am remembered for in this country? "The show was prepared before – Gary Lineker [one of the team captains] and the producer asked me to say that line all the time. It was just fun, but everybody took it seriously when it was just a joke and then when people don't want to listen, they don't listen.

"Gary Lineker and the producer were very kind to me after that. They said, 'We are very sorry, we didn't want that. It was just a fun part of the show.' But it's okay, I don't care. Time passed and I know what I did for Chelsea, and I cannot be resentful towards people in England because I had my best time there. Yes, it's true, I won the World Cup! But it's not the only thing that counts in my life. I'm not vain, I'm proud of being part of that team who made my country happy in '98, but I'm not that kind of guy."

That and the more aggressive soundbites which came out of Leboeuf's mouth might be the comments most supporters remember, but he was also a thoughtful player who channelled his own experiences to advise others. Having left his homeland to better himself as a footballer, he praised Steve McManaman for leaving his comfort zone in Liverpool to join Real Madrid, and encouraged more English footballers to follow their compatriot's lead by trading the Premier League for a club on the continent.

"If I say that, it's because I have the experience of what happened to me and to other [French] players," he explains. "We didn't win anything in 1982 and '86 at the World Cup because of a lack of experience of the players, who only played for some teams in France. When we went to other countries after the Bosman rule in 1995, we learned other cultures and we learned how to cope with other national teams. It helped us a lot to give us the experience to make sure we could become champions of the world."

He is particularly concerned at the lack of first-team opportunities for English players in the Premier League.

"You can see the problem you have right now with the national team. I remember after the first game when Sam Allardyce took over, he had only 70 players that he could pick a team from.

"It's just a pity because you have so many players with

qualities that it's just a shame that you don't see the strength and the quality of those players.

"If you cannot play in your country, go to another country and try to get this experience. Maybe you will have the chance to come back and play for a big club. Of course they want to stay in England; you have the money, everything. But maybe you need a little time to go to another country to learn a little bit more and come back as the real star. So that's why I said to Steve McManaman: 'Go – go there. You're going to learn, you'll win trophies, you're gonna play, you're gonna enjoy and you're going to show examples to all English players to go over and enjoy themselves.'"

What was the biggest lesson Leboeuf learned from his five years in England? It is the first question to halt the fast-talking Frenchman in his tracks.

"What it is to be a fan," he offers, before reiterating: "What it is to be a *real* fan. In all Latin countries, they are just there to see a show; to boo if they are not happy. What I like in England, when they are not happy they'd rather leave the stadium than boo the players. In France or Italy or Spain, people start insulting you, they berate you. You don't understand them. In England, you understand that you made a big mistake and you have to make sure you resolve the problem.

"In France football is a show, but in England it is a religion. In England, you feel football is created there. When you play at Wembley or any stadium in England, you can feel the passion, you can feel it's part of your genes and you see the seats are taken by the father and then the son and grandson. It's amazing. The atmosphere is really special.

"I had the chance, not too many times, when I was younger, to watch the FA Cup final. That was maybe the only game we could follow on TV. When Chelsea called me, I said, 'Oh my God, I have the opportunity to be in the country where football was created and I can feel, really feel, the atmosphere.' It really smashed me in the face. The first game we played was in the former stadium of Southampton, only 15,000 people, and I had to slap my face because I was watching the fans when I was in the middle of the pitch. 'Oh my God, what is that?!'

"I was amazed by the atmosphere at home with Chelsea because the club didn't win anything for like 25 years. Also, away from home, because fans are incredible all over England."

This fondness for English football is not unique to Leboeuf.

"I work now with Christophe Dugarry, Emmanuel Petit and William Gallas on the same TV show and we all share the same passion," he says. "Christophe only played in England for about a year and he said that is a regret for him. If he knew, he would have come to England earlier. But the other three of us had the time to enjoy the English fans, the songs. Everybody had a song and it's very special. You feel you are part of a family. It's something they have to carry on because I think footballers really appreciate it."

Leboeuf's song was a familiar one: "He's here, he's there, he's every-effing-where: Frank Leboeuf! Frank Leboeuf." In a radio interview, he expressed his joy at being the subject of a song by the supporters at Chelsea so early into his career with the club, while lamenting the profanity within it.

Cue the fans singing at the next home game: "He's here, he's there, we're not allowed to swear..." The mere mention of this brings a roar of laughter in approval.

"That was crazy! I said that on the radio and it was just a little message, but you don't think that all fans will listen to it and react so quickly. I heard the song and I just started laughing on the field. 'Oh my God, they're so freaking good.'"

Never before in his career had he experienced such a bond with those who paid their hard earned to watch his team. To be able to repay them with an FA Cup so early in his Chelsea career was a hugely gratifying moment.

"People always ask me the question, 'What is your best trophy?' Of course I put the World Cup, but I have to share the podium with the FA Cup in 1997 because it was absolutely perfect. The atmosphere, the win, the celebration after – we didn't want to leave Wembley and the fans didn't want to either. They had gone 27 years without winning the FA Cup, we felt this too, and we wanted to share the time with them. It wasn't only the 17 or 18 players and the club that won something, it's the population of the Chelsea fans who won it.

"The day after on the Fulham Road, that was... phwoar. I still have the pictures and I can still have the goosebumps if I think about it so much. You couldn't see the pavement that day because there were so many supporters. It was crazy. When we were close to the town hall of Fulham, I saw my father in the middle of it. I was on the bus and there was so many people, but I managed to pick him out – I still have that picture in my mind. This is stuff I will never forget from my time at Chelsea.

"For me, it is like yesterday. I still have the shirt. I sometimes look at the medal I have. It was my first trophy and I can't believe it's now 20 years ago. I feel like I am still there. It's true that sometimes I go to Stamford Bridge and people don't recognise me because the new generation don't know me. But for me, when I go back it is home sweet home."

The end of Leboeuf's time in west London coincided with the rise of John Terry, who has gone on the record to highlight the influence set by the Frenchman and his compatriot, Marcel Desailly. That it came at a time when Leboeuf had publicly fallen out with his manager says plenty about his character. There were times when he could have left Chelsea in the preceding summers, when first Gerard Houllier at Liverpool and then John Toshack at Real Madrid tried to sign him. His final season began with a public rebuke of Gianluca Vialli shortly before he was sacked.

At the time, the club was also said to be pursuing a move for Aston Villa centre-back Gareth Southgate and Leboeuf was expected to be the fall guy should the England international have made the move to west London. Laurent Blanc had also announced his imminent retirement from international football and his obvious successor was Leboeuf – but only if he was playing regularly.

Another light is shone on the situation when he describes his relationship with his former manager, which offers a little more context to his falling out with Vialli.

"Ruud and I were very close. I remember being injured when Zola played his first game at Blackburn. I called him up after the match. 'Ruud, how was Gianfranco?'

'He's very good. He's already there and he's going to be a big plus for us. Oh, Frank, we're coming back to London tonight, what are you doing?' I told him I was injured and I didn't think my coach would be very happy if I was going out with an injury. And do you know what he said? 'Well your coach is saying you'll meet him at the restaurant at 9pm. We're going to eat together and afterwards we'll go to a party.' 'Okay!'

"We were very close, like brothers almost. When he was fired he called me. 'I don't know what's going on, I don't know why they fired me. Can you come over.'

"I went over to his place and he wanted to call Ken Bates because 'Colin Hutchinson sacked me but maybe there is something to do with the chairman.'

"I said, 'Ruud, you've just been fired. I don't think Colin Hutchinson could decide that on his own. You are fired. You have to think about something else.'

"I never tried to know exactly what happened. It's just a pity because we had a very good atmosphere and it changed after that. Gianluca had more of an Italian style. I was very close to him [before his appointment] but of course he had to get away a little bit from our friendship, with me and also other players. With him we won the League Cup, Cup Winners' Cup and the Super Cup, and later the FA Cup, but the atmosphere wasn't the same.

"It was a difficult situation. They were both friends of mine and you feel sorry for one and happy for the other, but you know something happened behind and you don't really want to know because it's going to hurt you. The day after, I congratulated Gianluca but it was a strange feeling that we had all together, all friends. Roberto [Di Matteo], Gianluca, Dan [Petrescu] – we were all together and suddenly something changed and we said, 'Oh wow.' There are discussions that we had between each other and then you realise something has been discussed behind you as well. That makes the atmosphere different, of course.

"We don't talk any more together, which is a pity, but he made so many wrong comments or moves that made me think that he wasn't the same. It's more a pity for him than for me, but as I said he changed the atmosphere and for me the culture of my time at Chelsea will remain Ruud Gullit.

"I always say that was Ruud's team. Of course, Gianluca was

the coach, but we were on the way to the success. We had a good run and the club started to change with a new era. If Chelsea won the Premier League and Champions League, I want to say it was a little bit because of us, because we started the new era."

I have one final question to ask before our chat comes to an end. In light of his new career as an actor, what's more nerve-wracking, being on the pitch or on the stage?

"When you're on stage and facing the crowd, it's very intense," he responds. "But you cannot compare anything with sports. Sports, you don't know the end. It's uncertain every time you play. There is no script. You don't know where you go. You have opponents; people who don't like you in the crowd. It's complicated. It's a mental strength that you need but also stamina, focus, everything is complicated in sport. The feeling you have when you score a goal, or you win, or you get a trophy is incomparable to anything."

7. Dennis The Menace

*'I tried to never leave anything
in the tank. I played for the football
club, for the fans, because I love
football. And I had some fun
with them.'*

"Henry still cringes now. 'Dad, why did you do that?' Because I wanted you to share it with me, I tell him, and do you know the funny thing, H? Everyone actually started to like me after that because they thought I was human and that I was nice. The old dears really loved me, they all thought I wasn't as bad as everyone said. It's really funny because they'd only ever seen me on the pitch. People only take you by the image portrayed on the pitch."

Henry Wise is 17 years old, but to Chelsea supporters he will always be remembered as the infant who was proudly cradled in his father's right hand as he hoisted the FA Cup high into the Wembley sky with his left. He may cringe at the mere thought of it but Henry's place at the heart of the Blues' celebrations after beating Aston Villa, in the last final played at the old Wembley, confirmed to the wider football-watching public what Chelsea fans had known for years: Dennis Wise wasn't such a bad guy after all.

It didn't last, mind. Sixteen years on from his final appearance for this football club, he remains a divisive figure among English football supporters, but not here at Stamford Bridge, where he was the original Captain, Leader, Legend, as he forged a bond with the fans which continues to this day with every rendition of the famous "Oh, Dennis Wise" chant. He was the embodiment of the supporters on the pitch.

"I think they realised I'd given them everything," he says. "I tried to never leave anything in the tank. I think they appreciated that and they knew I had a real desire to win. I played for the football club, for the fans, because I love football. And I had some fun with them. I remember the game of head tennis in a game against Leicester when someone got injured – I threw the ball into the crowd, someone headed it back and

I headed it back to him. It was really funny and everyone was cheering me and this guy going back and forth with headers. I just wanted to share everything with the fans.

"When we won the FA Cup in '97, I made a point of getting a kid out of the crowd and I took him in the dressing room. I wanted the fans to enjoy the moment with us. They waited a long time and I just felt I wanted them to be part of it as well. I always did it – I'd grab a kid out of the crowd and walk him round, let him come in the changing room after the game, and then they'd go out to see their father at the tunnel. I remember one dad was crying his eyes out. Someone came in afterwards and told me the bloke wasn't crying because he was so happy for his son, it was because he hadn't come in and celebrated with us!"

Nothing made him prouder than winning trophies for Chelsea, but at the start of the 1996/97 season, Wise was a frustrated player. He loved playing for, and captaining, a club he had taken to his heart over the previous six years, but there was something missing: silverware. At the time, the list of captains to lift a trophy for Chelsea made for pretty short reading; limit the criteria to major honours won at Wembley Stadium and there was no need for even a scrap of paper. So, when he signed a new contract in the winter of 1996, which was thought to be the first by a British player to take them into the 21st century, Wise had only one thing on his mind: "I want to win something. I don't want someone to say he had great times here but he never won anything. I want my photo up on the wall and punters saying, 'Yeah, we won this with him, we won that.' I want it to be like it is with Peter Osgood, people remembering him for what he won."

When he joined Chelsea in 1990 he had already tasted

success with his former club Wimbledon, where he had been part of the Crazy Gang which upset Liverpool's Culture Club, as John Motson put it, in the 1988 FA Cup final. The Blues had to pay a club-record fee to convince the Dons to part with their midfielder just a few years after we had spurned the opportunity to add him to the junior ranks following his release from Southampton.

Wise had seen Chelsea change dramatically in the space of only a few years. He, too, had changed with them, although perhaps not quite as drastically as the club itself. Cynics would say his Chelsea career was perfectly encapsulated by his first two appearances, when he followed up a man-of-the-match performance on his debut against Derby County, in which he had provided telling cross after telling cross for the Blues' grateful strikeforce, with a red card against Crystal Palace a few days later following a scrap with Andy Gray. The reality was there were far more instances of the former than the latter, and a better example of what Wise was all about came a couple of years into his 11-year stint with the Blues.

In February 1992, Chelsea travelled up to Anfield without a league victory at the home of the Reds for more than half a century. The mischievous Wise, along with his old partner in crime, Vinnie Jones, scrawled "We're bothered" over the "This is Anfield sign" in the tunnel. They backed up their words by both scoring in a famous win. Wise, who finished as our leading scorer in the league that season, marked his goal by rushing over to the away end to celebrate with the supporters. To me, that is Dennis Wise: cheeky and passionate, but with the quality to make a difference on the pitch. The aggressive, terrier-like midfielder, who Sir Alex Ferguson once suggested was capable of starting a row in an empty house, was our loveable rogue, the heart and soul of the football club. If he was on your side, you loved him, but when the shoe was on the other foot...

"My idol as a youngster was Dennis Wise," boyhood Blues fan, and a fellow Player of the Year winner at the club, Joe Cole once said. "I got the chance to play against him when I was at West Ham and he never stopped giving me stick, he was in my ear all game: 'You're rubbish, you can't pass the ball, you can't do nothing.' After about 60 minutes I absolutely lumped him!"

Sometimes Wise's passion boiled over, however, and you didn't often have to look too far to find him if it was all kicking off on the pitch. Shortly before the aforementioned contract renewal, he and Ruud Gullit had discussed what the latter described as Wise's "Crazy Gang mindset" and how he perceived his captain's will to win manifesting itself in the form of incidents which were avoidable. He felt Wise was a far better player than he was given credit for and such flare-ups on the pitch were doing a disservice to him.

"He wanted me to manage the way I was in a better way, which meant I could play more games and be on the field more," Wise says. "I get what he was saying, but there was a balance between taking a bit away from somebody and not. We argued about the whole thing a little bit and at the end of the day it was fine, we ended up speaking and he left me out to prove a point to me. It probably taught me a little lesson and that was good, because I knew I had to curb the way I played a little bit to try and help the team. He wanted to play football and he knew I could do it.

"He didn't want this image that was always portrayed of me. Unfortunately I'd got it during the early part of my career at

Wimbledon and it doesn't change, people don't think about the good play, but it's just, 'He gets stuck in, he'll put his foot in'. Unfortunately we're all put in different categories, and it didn't really bother me, to be honest. I was there to do a job for the team and to work tirelessly for the individuals in the midfield and to protect the back four. I had to do my job for the team and it wasn't as glamorous as some of the others. You couldn't ask Franco to do what I did but you couldn't ask me to do what Franco did. I just had to manage it better and that's the conversation me and Ruud had."

The story above also highlighted another important facet of his captaincy, which was his willingness to speak openly with his managers, in particular Gullit and Gianluca Vialli. Wearing the armband meant so much to him and he was an old-school leader in the sense that he knew the name of every player in the reserves and the youth team, as well as those working behind the scenes at the club, but also in the way he was never afraid to speak his mind. It didn't matter whether it was to the manager or a star player, on or off the pitch, if something needed to be said then he would say it. In one match at QPR, he had been frustrated by the lack of urgency Gullit, yet to be promoted into the dugout, had shown to his defensive duties. "Oi, Ruudi, get your arse back here," he screamed, loud enough that it could be heard in the stands at Loftus Road.

"I think the fact I was a player with them and I'd become friends with them made it easier," Wise reflects. "When they came in, I helped them, so it was probably easier for me to talk to them and chat to them, and I had no hesitation speaking to Ruud or Luca. If you've got something to say, they were always willing to listen. They wanted your feedback. If there are problems, you try to sort them out. Everyone has their own thought processes and I think what happens in football is that a lot of players don't want to make that approach, but it's probably better to have a one-to-one and get your feelings out of your system. I was one that tried to be as honest as I could with the manager. Whether it was good, bad or ugly, so be it."

He captained the club for eight years, give or take a brief spell when Glenn Hoddle took the armband away from him after disciplinary problems on and off the pitch, and even then the man who replaced him as skipper, Gavin Peacock, recalls a conversation when Wise told him there was "no issue" between them.

That selfless leadership was on show later on when he beckoned Vialli to collect the Coca-Cola Cup trophy after a win over Middlesbrough in which Wise had been named man of the match and the new player-manager had surprisingly opted to only fulfil the latter part of his duties despite being in excellent goalscoring form in his second season at the club. "We just felt he should go up himself because we all felt he should be part of it," he said at the time. That was the Wise mantra. The team was always at the forefront of his thinking, which contributed to him leading them out on 298 occasions, a tally surpassed only by John Terry and Ron Harris. Indeed, he was our most successful captain prior to JT.

During the latter part of his Blues career, Wise was the leader of a team in which he was often the only Englishman playing. As the Nineties was entering its final week, Chelsea became the first English club to field an all-foreign starting XI when we defeated Southampton 2-0 on Boxing Day 1999. Wise was absent to attend the birth of his son, and in the side that day were two Italians, Gabriele Ambrosetti and Roberto

Di Matteo, alongside two Frenchmen, Frank Leboeuf, Didier Deschamps, Dutch goalkeeper Ed de Goey, Spanish right-back Albert Ferrer, Brazilian centre-back Emerson Thome, Nigerian left-back Celestine Babayaro, Romanian right-winger Dan Petrescu, Uruguayan central midfielder Gus Poyet and Norwegian centre-forward Tore Andre Flo, who scored both Chelsea goals.

The result probably helped to dampen what could have been an almighty storm, although there was still some consternation among the press corps, who were worried about the implications for the future. Wise doesn't see the fuss.

"I think I was probably there many times on my own as the only English boy in the side. It doesn't matter if you're English or you're a foreigner. It really doesn't. What matters is what's inside the group. We're all different individuals but it's about your passion for the football club. I wanted us to win and we all shared that mentality, whether you were playing or not. That's important inside the group, that every individual wants you to win. We had a good group, we were fortunate the individuals were very professional and very close together."

There was more than just good fortune involved. At the heart of it all was a Wise man whose name was a regular feature in a recent matchday programme series called Team-mates, in which nearly every player interviewed who featured for Chelsea during the mid-to-late Nineties picked him out as the best leader they played alongside. He was the glue that bonded everyone together, forging a team spirit that would see the club enjoy its most prosperous period before the Roman Abramovich era gave us a whole new level of success that was beyond most supporters' wildest dreams.

"How did I do it? To give you an example, Luca Vialli was

on his own when he first came over and what I didn't want was to leave him on his own, to sit in and not do anything. Me and Claire [Wise's wife] weren't too far away from where he lived so we'd take him to the pictures on a Friday or go out for something to eat together. It was important for everyone to mix together, to understand each other, to be part of everything that was going on. One thing I don't like is leaving people on their own, so I tried to make a point that if any one individual was on their own, I'd help them out.

"It was important to make people feel welcome. They've come from a different country, a different environment, they want to learn the culture and don't fully understand it, and you don't want the fans to get on their back, you don't want them to have a bad time – you want them to be relaxed and to do the best for themselves, because if they do that, they're going to do the best for us. And that's what is best for the football club. That's how it was. There was no trying to point people out and make them scapegoats, we were all in it together. We won together and we failed together. That was it. We all make mistakes, but it's about helping each other to not worry about those types of things.

"I also made everyone speak English. That was important inside the dressing room. If you had a problem or you wanted to say something, it was important for everyone to understand it. We were lucky enough to have some very talented players, and very caring people within the group. You've only got to look at Robbie, Luca, Franco, Dan, Gus and people like that – they understood. They're nice people in general, so they get it, that understanding. We just seemed to hit it off, the combination of us together – English, Italian, Romanian, Uruguayan, French, whatever – just all thinking on the same wavelength. We all wanted to achieve certain things, but we also all wanted to look after the group, and that doesn't just mean the squad of players. The group included the staff – the kitchen lady, kit men, all the way through – and it was about looking after everyone. I wanted everyone to come in and enjoy coming to work. It was important that they enjoyed it because that's how you're going to get the best out of people."

And he made them sing. The now customary tradition of new signings standing up in front of the rest of the group to belt out a rendition of a song of their choice was introduced on Wise's watch.

"I just thought it would be really funny to hear the foreigners sing a song, especially if their English was broken. So I said to them, 'Look, guys, we have a tradition here...' I just made it up. I got all the new boys to start singing and it took off. But first of all I made the kids sing – they used to do it at Christmas and they'd serve us and sing as well. It was a laugh, it was enjoyable. You can play in front of 100,000 people and do incredible things on a football pitch, but I've never seen Franco as worried as when he had to go up in front of the lads to sing a song! That was the dreaded thing, more nerve-wracking than anything they'd been through in their career. 'Please, please Dennis. No, no.' Sorry, Franco, you have to sing – it's tradition. He wasn't even the worst, there were some really bad ones – Robbie stands out. And Frode shocked everyone when he jumped up on the table, he was like a madman. But do you know what, it shows different personalities and it brings people out. It makes people laugh."

Wise asks if I've ever heard the story about Grappler. It's a tale that illustrates perfectly the bond within the group at that time.

"Grappler was a guy called Alex Nairn and he was our masseur. He's passed away now, bless him, and I went to his funeral. I used to come in early and he'd give me a massage. We were always joking around, but one day he flipped. He had a problem which we didn't know about – he didn't have a lot of money and he'd just paid £1,000 to fix his car and then it broke down again. We had a little argument and then I found out what had happened. I didn't want Grappler coming in every morning feeling sad and under pressure because of this. I wanted him to enjoy himself.

"There was a group of lads – Graeme Le Saux, Gus, Robbie, Franco – and I said, 'Guys, there's an issue here. Shall we buy him a car from the players' pool?' We used to use this money to donate to charity, look after the staff, stuff like that. So we bought him a brand-new Skoda that had just come out. We got it delivered to the training ground and tied a bow around it. I had the car keys in my pocket and I said, 'Grappler, I need your help getting something out of my car.' He walked outside and I followed him. All the lads were standing in front of the car and they slowly separated to reveal it. I said, 'Look, we've bought you a car.' And he started crying. He gave all the lads a big cuddle and then we're all taking the pee out of him for crying! We gave him the £1,000 he'd lost as well. That was the group of lads we had. He was struggling and he needed help – the guys were always there to help. Always looking for a solution."

That applied on the pitch, too, and Wise feels his best football was played predominantly under Vialli, who utilised him in a deeper midfield role which made the most of his underrated technical abilities and his tenacity, while also utilising the primary attributes of the other three players who made up one of the best midfields in Chelsea's history. Lining up in a diamond shape, he sat at the base with Dan Petrescu on one side and Gustavo Poyet on the other, and Roberto Di Matteo stationed at the tip. The other three often rotated position, but Wise was the constant; the heartbeat of the side in more ways than one. Twice he won the Player of the Year award in that time, in 1998 and 2000, although he also received six red cards in two seasons – three in 1998/99, plus another in a pre-season match at Atletico Madrid that ruled him out of three Premier League matches, and two dismissals the following campaign – which perhaps indicated the "Crazy Gang mentality" hadn't fully departed.

"I think between 1997 and 2000 was the time I probably played my best football, but I never got picked by England during that period – and that was Glenn. We were different personalities, but we won't go into that! Let's also not forget I had Paul Gascoigne and Paul Ince in front of me at the time, and there was Paul Scholes as well, so that's probably the reason why. It wasn't a bad midfield, was it? But I didn't even get into any squads. It was Kevin Keegan who brought me back in and I played at the Euros in 2000."

He appeared in all three matches of England's ill-fated campaign – the Three Lions were eliminated in the group stages – although he was one of the few players to emerge with any credit after a dogged performance in a 1-0 win over Germany. However, his international career ended later that year after 21 caps and a solitary goal, both modest tallies for a player who had so much to offer.

It is almost forgotten that he was once the top-scoring midfielder in Chelsea's history – his tally of 76 goals only surpassed by Frank Lampard – and perhaps his most famous strike came against AC Milan in our first Champions League campaign. When a goal is celebrated in song by supporters for many years after the event, we can deduce that it was either a vital strike or a worldie. Wise's goal at the San Siro certainly fell into the former category, but its quality should not be underestimated either. The pass from Roberto Di Matteo, clipped over the top, picked out an intelligent run from Chelsea's No11 in between Paolo Maldini and Roberto Ayala, two world-class defenders; the touch with his right to kill the ball was matched by a clinical left-footed shot through the legs of the goalkeeper. Wise is typically understated in his appraisal of the moment he announced himself as a player of Champions League quality.

"It was a good ball by Robbie, a good run, good touch and good finish. But it was more about who we were playing against: the mighty Milan. It was important because it gave us an edge over them and I think we won the group – well, that's what won us the group in my opinion. We'd have had a different pathway otherwise."

But it wasn't just what the goal meant for our Champions League hopes that season, although at the time that was all that mattered as it put us in pole position to finish ahead of the Italian side. Rather, it was what it symbolised, ushering in a new era at Chelsea.

Five years earlier, when the Blues had reached the FA Cup final for the first time in 24 years, we finished 14th in the Premier League and had been battling relegation at Christmas, while AC Milan had lifted the European Cup for the fifth time. It was beyond fanciful to suggest the two sides would meet in the Champions League, let alone for the Blues to match them twice in the group stage. In the end, we finished five points clear of the Rossoneri to top the group. Earlier that month, we also defeated the reigning Champions League holders Manchester United at Stamford Bridge; not just beaten, but battered into submission, a 5-0 drubbing the least our dazzling performance deserved. The times they were a-changin'. And though most fans were quite satisfied with a thrilling run in Europe's premier club competition which ended at the quarter-finals, for Wise his sole campaign mixing it with the elite sides on the continent is tinged with regret.

In his programme notes ahead of the home leg against Barcelona – when, in Wise's words, "We absolutely stormed them" – he wrote: "In my first FA Cup game for Chelsea we lost 3-1 at home to Oxford United. Now it's Barcelona at home, Newcastle at Wembley in the FA Cup semi-final and later Barcelona away. We've come a long way, you and us, haven't we?"

It was a sign of just how far Chelsea had progressed that a two-legged defeat to Barcelona could be considered a disappointment. To most supporters, the Catalans were a mythical side, like gods from another planet. And here were our boys mixing it with them as if they were equals.

"Look, you always dream about playing in the Champions League, you always hope it's going to happen. I think when I first walked into that football club there was no chance. You've only got to look at the personnel that played, and it's no disrespect to them, but you can only go to a certain level with the group that we had then. Once you start to get different personnel in, then you look at the group within and you go, 'We've got a chance here. We've got a chance in everything.'

"The fact is, we were going through to the semi-final with five minutes to go and then Bernard Lambourde slipped from the free-kick and they scored, which put us into extra time and we ended up going out.

"We had a couple of those situations in my latter years at the club, which you look back on and see we were so close, but we just needed that little extra – maybe a bit of luck to go our way. We had a similar scenario in the Cup Winners' Cup which still haunts me now. We played Mallorca in the semi-final in 1999, when we were the holders, and no team had won the competition twice on the trot. Zola had the ball out wide. I got into the box; my timing was spot on and his ball was spot on, but my heading was c**p! It was right at the end of the game. I changed my mind – I should have headed it and I tried to flick it and it just skimmed the post. I looked at Luca and just collapsed onto my knees. I knew it was such a big opportunity to help us have a chance of achieving something really special. And I missed. That moment stayed with me, it annoyed me immensely. Things stick in your mind.

"In the dressing room after the Barcelona game, Bernard was sitting there with his hands over his head and he was sobbing. He felt he'd let us down. It wasn't just his responsibility, you can't account for him slipping. You go back – why did we give the free-kick away? Why did we give the ball away? It's a collective problem, not just one individual sometimes. He knew we were so close to getting a big result at Barcelona. It hurt him. These things we remember. They're times that are really disappointing."

Another regret is when the Blues finished just four points behind Premier League champions Manchester United, who went on to win the FA Cup and Champions League in the 1998/99 season.

"We should have won the league but we ballsed it up against

West Ham (0-1 defeat) and Leicester (2-2 after leading 2-0). I missed something like 12 games that season through suspension. That's what really, really, really annoyed me. I was so disappointed to miss so many games. Would I have made the difference? Who knows. But I was annoyed with myself because I remember sitting and watching the West Ham game up in the stands and I'm thinking, 'Come on guys, come on.' I was playing in the match against Leicester, and we were two up with nine minutes to go. Steve Guppy [who scored the equaliser] will never, ever hit one like that again on his right foot. Never."

Of course, it wasn't the 'if only' moments which defined Wise's Chelsea career. The photos of him are up on the wall; punters can say we won this and we won that with him. To Blues supporters, he was our representation on the pitch and the canny leader who finally – finally! – brought silverware back to Stamford Bridge, starting with that magical FA Cup triumph in 1997 which just felt like destiny.

"After losing in the final in 1994, I believed we were going to win it this time," he says. "We all kind of knew it, and you do *know*. But the relief I felt afterwards... I sat down and there was just this massive feeling of satisfaction that came over me. It's really difficult to explain. It felt like such an achievement, kind of like: 'Do you know what? We've done something here and it's been a long, long time and I'm so pleased we've achieved this.' And it was for everyone, really. Obviously the fans, but also for Batesy and his wife Suzannah, and for all the staff. It was a great moment for everyone.

"Honestly, it's such a wonderful feeling to walk up those steps to collect the trophy. You get up there so quickly and actually I think we probably enjoyed it more in 2000 because we got up there, we celebrated, we'd done what he had to do, but we didn't take enough in. When you get to the next one it's like, 'Guys, we've got to *really* enjoy this one.' In 2000, we really did. It was different to '97, when we went into the game and knew how long we hadn't won something for. This one we were going into it having won quite a few trophies, so the mentality is a bit different.

"This time, I said to the guys, 'Let's grab our kids and take them up.' It was just spur of the moment. The people around you, your family and friends, go through all this with you – the good times, the pain, the lot – and they need to share it with you as well and be part of it. That's the way I am, I'll never change."

Little did any of us know, this was the last hurrah for many of the players who made Chelsea great again, and a year later Wise was one of a number of senior players moved on. Gone, but not forgotten. When he returned to Stamford Bridge as an opposition player for Leicester City in October 2001, the 2-0 victory for the Blues was largely an afterthought. Wise's name was sung by all four sides of Stamford Bridge prior to kick-off, almost drowning out the words of chairman Ken Bates as he attempted to pay tribute to a genuine Blues legend. The midfielder was cheered throughout the match, although it was the supporters' reaction to his first foul of the match which Wise appreciated most. A chant of, "Off, off off!" brought a smile to his face and perfectly illustrated the bond between player and fans which had been built over the previous 11 years. After the final whistle he stayed out to acknowledge his beloved supporters.

"I can look back on my time at Chelsea and say I thoroughly enjoyed every moment," Wise says. "There were some ups and a few downs, but they were the best years of my career. I absolutely loved it and my team is Chelsea. I spent a long time there and I grew with that club. It meant a lot, it's precious to me, and it's something that will always stick in my mind. I had some lovely times there and there is so much to talk about."

His legacy at the football club didn't end that day; it is felt every single time John Terry takes to the field as skipper. As a young boy learning his trade in the youth team, JT used to clean Wise's boots and his reward was far more gratifying than the tip he would receive every Christmas, or the few quid he would receive when the boots he had cleaned helped Wise find the back of the net to earn himself a goal bonus.

"In terms of captains, Dennis would be the instant one for me that I looked up to," said Terry in an interview with the Chelsea website a few years ago. "Being in and around him, even when I wasn't part of the first team, you could see the impact he had. You always heard him, being on the training pitch next to him, and he was always motivating people. And just the way he trained as well, because sometimes people think being captain is about being the loudest, being this, but sometimes it's setting the right precedent and training the right way so that everyone follows suit. When he spoke in the dressing room at half-time and stuff, people obviously listened to Wisey, and being a young kid around that you got to see it.

"I think he definitely had that about him. He was by far the main one. Even around the dressing room, he brought people together. He didn't let younger players take the mick, and kept everyone in check – myself, at times, as well. He was really close to me and took me under his wing as well. I learnt an awful lot from him. He doesn't like it when I say to him, 'Listen, I looked up to you as my hero and to get to clean your boots…' He's a little bit humbled by it: 'Leave it, leave it.' He doesn't want to go into it. But that's him: he didn't try and be a captain."

He never tried to be something he wasn't – and Chelsea supporters loved him all the more because of it.

8. Viking Warrior

'When you arrive at the stadium and you
see blue everywhere you look, it hits you.
I was thinking: "Don't mess it up today!
If I do that, I'll have to move back to
Norway, into the fjords, and find a cabin
to stay in for the rest of my life."'

"Every Saturday at 4pm," begins Frode Grodas, who has briefly been transported back to the Seventies. The crackly phone line which connects us from his home in Norway merely accentuates the nostalgic scene he is setting. "Every single Saturday. That was the highlight, that was our window to see the big guys. Everybody had their favourite team, but not me; I only had my favourite player, Peter Shilton. I never picked a team because he changed all the time. Nottingham Forest were very good and when he was there they won the league and two European Cups. I remember that team very well."

To illustrate the global appeal of the Premier League, one need only look at the money expected to be brought in by the overseas television deal for the three seasons beginning from 2016/17: a cool £3 billion, up from the £2.2 billion for the previous three campaigns. That figure is largely driven by the US and Chinese markets, where English football clubs are regular visitors on pre-season tours, but matches are shown in 212 territories across the globe and it is undoubtedly the most-watched football league in the world.

In Norway, the roots beneath the love of English football run far deeper than most. The Scandinavian country, with a population of just over five million, may not be able to match other countries' viewing figures and spending power, but their fascination with the English game goes way back to the 1920s, when the Norwegian daily press began covering it, and it intensified with live matches from these shores televised every weekend from 1969, a good 10 years before the same coverage was offered by ITV. It has long since overtaken the domestic top flight as the most popular league in the country. According to a 2010 study by Visit Britain, one in 13 Norwegian tourists visits England specifically to attend a Premier League match. Even Harald V, the King of Norway, supports an English football club. Pity for him, then, that it is Tottenham Hotspur.

"I can't really explain how big English football is in Norway," Grodas says. "The fans are completely crazy about it. I have a son who is a Chelsea supporter and I try to calm him down when they are playing, but the fans here are completely out of their minds when it comes to English football. They are brainwashed by it. And the FA Cup is something you wait for the whole year. It's really difficult to describe the feelings we have for English football. It's strange. I played some of my career in Germany and it's also a great league with massive teams – but it's nothing in Norway, it's not interesting at all."

Chelsea's Norway Supporters' Club is based out of Oslo and will soon be celebrating its 40th anniversary, having been founded in 1980 – comfortably the earliest of our official European supporters' clubs. It now boasts 1,300 members, which is a ratio of more than 400 for every Norwegian player who has represented the Blues, all of them across an 11-year period from 1989 to 2000, when Scandinavia was one of the primary exporters to the English top flight.

The first, Erland Johnsen, can lay claim to being the first overseas player to appear for the Blues in a Premier League match, doing so in a 3-0 defeat at Nottingham Forest on 16 January 1993. The most recent, Tore Andre Flo, scored 50 goals for the club and returned post-playing to take up a coaching role in the Academy. In between you have Grodas, who spent the least amount of time at the club at a little over a year and appeared in only 27 matches, comfortably the fewest of the trio. But Freddie, as Dennis Wise used to call him, did something that eluded both of his peers, and indeed his boyhood hero: he started an FA Cup final, and in doing so became the second of only four goalkeepers – as of the start of the 2016/17 season – to emerge victorious for the Blues. Peter Bonetti, Ed de Goey and Petr Cech complete the list.

Grodas is comfortably the least heralded of that quartet and, indeed, of our 1997 FA Cup-winning team. He arrived as a 32-year-old unknown on these shores to try to solve the question which had plagued Chelsea supporters for the best part of a decade: can we please have a reliable goalkeeper? A whole host of custodians attempted to be the answer in the wake of the knee injury which cut short the career of Eddie Niedzwiecki, the most noteworthy of whom were Dave Beasant, Kevin Hitchcock and Dmitri Kharine. All three had their moments, but consistent excellence eluded each of them. Bes was the subject of an Ian Porterfield rant after a couple of clangers against Norwich City in an early Premier League match, the Blues manager declaring he would not play for the club again. He did, after Porterfield became the first manager sacked in the era of the rebranded English top flight, but then an unfortunate incident involving a jar of salad cream and his foot proved to be one mishap too many. Hitchy perhaps fell victim to his status as the loyal back-up, with the number of non-playing substitute appearances comfortably doubling the amount of times he made it onto the pitch. And Kharine, for all his excellence, was just a little bit too, in the words of club historian Rick Glanvill, "windy" for a goalkeeper.

Grodas was not the long-term answer, though the sample size for this conclusion is far smaller than the others, and it is telling that he, along with Hitchcock, Kharine, Nick Colgan and Craig Forrest, was one of five goalkeepers to be used in the 1996/97 season, which remains a club record for a single campaign. Ruud Gullit was unconvinced and one of his first acts of the summer following the FA Cup win was to recruit the services of De Goey. It would be unfair to suggest the affable Norwegian was simply in the right place at the right moment in order to write his name in Chelsea's history, but he was certainly the goalkeeper who found form at the key time. That he was even in a position to do so is something of a miracle in itself when you hear of his journey to Wembley.

"We lived in a small part of the west of Norway, in the fjords, only 1,200 people in the village," Grodas says. "My father was a goalkeeper, but I never saw him play and he never trained me because we had a shop – and the main thing for him was that I was going to work there. He didn't see the importance of training. But I have three brothers, two of them older, and they are the reason I became a goalie. They needed someone to shoot at! I was the number three kid and I had to be their goalkeeper.

"There was actually only one goalkeeper in the village, so I started training with the first team when I was eight years old. I got my debut when I was 12! I wasn't big but I wasn't small, so I was okay. I was playing for Hornindal, which is famous for having the deepest fresh-water sea in north Europe. And that's where I am from.

"As kids we would play up in the mountains, I remember volleyball and skiing. I loved to go up the top of the mountain and ski. We were active all the time with different sports. But I had no chance to become a skier. We had to make our own hills, there were no lifts or anything. When you don't have parents who will take you around Norway to all the training competitions, you have no chance. And it was much the same with football. Our team didn't have a coach and I certainly never had a goalkeeping coach before I was 25. You couldn't even play football from November to March. To travel from my home and my upbringing all the way to Wembley in 1997 is a journey that shouldn't be possible. No one from that village had managed to come out and play [in the top flight] in Norway or abroad. No one around me believed you could become a football player and I didn't believe it either."

He became a big story in his village, but not even winning the FA Cup and helping Norway to the last 16 of the 1998 World Cup, which remains their best tournament showing, was enough to keep him at the top of the mountain.

"I don't know if you know ski jumping, apart from Eddie the Eagle. Well, the world-record holder is my nephew, Anders Fannemel! He had a father who took him around to train and compete. If you don't have this support around you, there is no chance. He did – and he really made it. I don't know how far he jumped... 200... 250 metres... I should know that!

"My son, Victor, is also a footballer. Not a goalkeeper but a left-back. He has also won a cup final, but in Norway. He did something I didn't do. He's now playing for my first professional team, Sogndal, but at the time he was playing for Hødd. They were really down in the First Division but they went all the way through, a surprising team. They beat Tromso, the European opponent for Chelsea many years ago in the snow match."

Speaking with Grodas, it is easy to see how he quickly became one of the boys at Chelsea. He is easy to talk to, sharp witted and with a dry sense of humour. Like his compatriot Johnsen, who he believes is "90 per cent Englishman", he enjoyed a drink and never took himself too seriously. Rumour has it that at his first Chelsea Christmas party, the two Norwegians chased Gianfranco Zola and tried to force the teetotal Italian to drink a glass of Vodka.

"No, no, no," Grodas responds. "It was not vodka – it was Cognac! But he didn't drink it. We really tried because we thought it would be good for his muscles, it would help him grow. He didn't agree. It's a funny story, though. I didn't even know he didn't drink. It took him a while to trust me after that!"

Gullit aside, who he fell out with towards the end of his time at the club, he has kind words for all of his old team-mates, but the most affection is shown towards Johnsen and it is a friendship which remains just as strong today. No longer team-mates, the two men are now colleagues within the Norwegian FA, working at the Ullevaal Stadion in Oslo, which is the country's national stadium.

"I work with the young goalkeepers and he has just signed a new two-year contract coaching the Under-15 and Under-17 boys national team. Chelsea is shaping the future of Norwegian football! We have another guy, Gunnar Halle, who you might also remember from English football at that time. He has the Under-16s. I have to say, in some ways English football was more professional than what we were used to and the level of the players was much higher, but we had a national team at that time that was very good – a lot of personalities – and you can see the guys leading or coaching in Norwegian football now are all coming from this national team.

"With Erland, I knew him before I signed for Chelsea and we are also about the same age. He told me all the stories about what the club was like in his early years there and it sounded like nothing I had ever experienced. He told a story about Kerry Dixon in training and them hitting each other and beating each other! Then after training they shook hands and it was nothing personal, they left it behind. I think it must have been a very tough team at that time!

"When I arrived he was already well adapted to life there. From my point of view, I have to say it's something good when you come to a new country and a new club and you know some things – where to go, who to talk to, how to organise things. It made it much easier and he made my life easier. I could call him if ever I didn't know anything. He presented me with the network he had around him and you adapt much faster at a club when you know someone. We became very close and we still are today."

Grodas did the same thing with Tore Andre Flo when he joined the club in the summer of 1997, opening up his house in Ascot to the striker – "It was fine then because he didn't have five kids!" – during an era when assistance for foreign players coming over to England was nothing like it is today, although in Mark Hughes's eyes it compared favourably to what he experienced with Barcelona in the Eighties. The training ground certainly made things easier with its close proximity to Heathrow and, in fact, a trip to London remains the first and only time Grodas's mother has ever travelled by plane, a journey she undertook at the age of 72. All that was missing for the Norwegian players to feel right at home was Brunost, the country's iconic brown cheese.

"That is something we Norwegians must bring with us, it doesn't matter where we go," Grodas insists. "The cheese is made from goats' milk and it is quite sweet. But it tastes fantastic, especially with fresh bread and coffee. Heaven. I eat that every day. The other thing I really missed was honey. I produce my own now – goalkeeping honey! There are actually around 120,000 bees who are 20 metres away from where I am sitting now. I'm not joking."

The settling in process might not have been as straight-forward had things panned out differently for Grodas in the late Eighties, when he was performing out of his skin for Lillestrom, who at the time were managed by former Chelsea and Scotland midfielder David Hay. He was twice invited over to England for trials – possibly arranged as a result of his manager's contacts within the English game, although Grodas is unsure – and on both occasions he returned home disappointed.

"David was a very good man," he says. "I didn't know much about his history with Chelsea because he didn't talk about it, or himself, he talked about football and you. He really lifted my training with his high expectations and at Lillestrom we won the league with him in 1989.

"I'd had two fantastic seasons and at the time I was really, really good. I was disappointed I didn't get a chance to play in a bigger league at that time, but it was before the Bosman ruling and it was more difficult for goalkeepers to get out. It was easier for goalscorers. They take all the headlines!

"But the dream lived on. There were people, agents, who said teams were interested and I went over for a trial at Southampton, but I didn't really feel they needed a goalkeeper. To go on trial – with new players, facilities, a different way of playing, foreign language, the culture, all of this – is quite unnatural. You need a little bit of luck. I was wanted by West Ham as well and Lou Macari was the manager, but it was the same thing. I am a person who needs a little time to adapt. Sometimes you don't have that. Maybe with the right coach I could have done something at that time."

Instead, he had to wait almost a decade to finally make the move, by which time he was an established international. He didn't have time to adapt, really, and the coach certainly wasn't the right one in his eyes. But the stars aligned for that short and sweet period, allowing him to fulfil a lifelong ambition by winning the most famous domestic cup competition of them all. When I ask him for the first thing that comes to mind when he thinks back to the FA Cup triumph, the response is almost instant.

"Wembley is what made the FA Cup final so special," he says. "You hear about it from almost the first time you ever touch a football. That was my first time there. In the dressing room before the game, I knew we were the better team and I just had a feeling that it was going to be our day – I think it was when I looked over at Sparky and he was eating some stones and ripping out parts of the wall! The early goal by Robbie just backed that up. I didn't have too many saves to make in that game, I can only remember maybe a header and a one-against-one in the second half, but it wasn't the busiest day of my career.

"And, of course, I remember wearing the Viking helmet after the game. I even gave Ruud Gullit a hug – I never did it before or after that day! All of the joy, the screaming – you just don't know what to do with yourself. There are so many feelings throughout the day. It's something to remember for the rest of your life, you have to store a picture of it all in your memory. I have the game on DVD and I've seen it a couple of times. My son has also watched it with me, but he gets furious when I remind him that he had the chance to go to the final. Instead, he chose to stay home. He regrets that. I think he was only six years old and he was playing football in the garden with his mate Jack. That was his FA Cup final and Wembley Stadium..."

Then he stops. His voice takes on a more sombre tone as he relays to me a story about how he thought his Wembley dream would remain just that – a dream.

"I actually thought I wasn't going to be able to play in it. We took on Everton in the last game before the final and I got a red card. My first thought was that, because of how the disciplinary procedures worked in Norway, I was going to miss the Cup final. I was completely broken; I was crying when I went into the dressing room. Luckily for me, things worked a little bit differently in England at that time and the suspension didn't come in straight away. I only found out in the evening when we were coming back to London on the bus. The players saw I was a little bit down, we talked about it, and then I just shouted out because I was so, so happy!

"In the build-up to the game, you are in the hotel and that keeps you away from the pressure of it. But when you arrive at the stadium and you see blue everywhere you look, it hits you. And it's at that point, when I was in the tunnel, that I had a thought: 'Don't mess it up today! If I do that, I'll have to move back to Norway, into the fjords, and find a cabin to stay in for the rest of my life.' That was the last thought I had before going onto the pitch. Luckily, I didn't mess it up."

And so we were treated to the sight of Grodas in his Viking helmet, dancing on the Wembley turf and celebrating the greatest triumph of his life – the triumph that shouldn't have been possible. He owes much of that to Johnsen, whose last-minute tumble against Leicester City in the fifth round replay provided the penalty kick for Frank Leboeuf to win the tie.

"I think he lost his balance," Grodas dryly observes, "He's a big guy so it's quite easy for that to happen. At that time, Stamford Bridge's pitch wasn't as flat as it is now so it could happen to anyone..."

While that incident was written into Chelsea folklore, Grodas had calmly repelled a physical Leicester attack, just as he helped to blunt Wimbledon's Crazy Gang in the semi-final. In fact, of the five appearances he made during the Cup run, Portsmouth's Deon Burton was the only player to beat him, and that was little more than a consolation in a 4-1 win in the sixth round.

"Very physical," is his assessment of the challenges he was confronted by. "Leicester at that time was a great team, but very physical. I remember having a crash with Ian Marshall, a real crash! It was a tough game. So, when you struggle and you manage to get through that with a goal in the last minutes, it's fantastic. I remember Steve Clarke, in the shower, telling us, 'We're going to win the FA Cup this year.' He really believed it and it gave us all so much confidence. He was so convincing. He said a lot of things you wouldn't always listen to, but at that minute it was something which burned into us. And he was right.

"When we played Wimbledon, obviously I was aware of them. We had Erland playing for us in that match and he was very important, but I clearly remember the first cross in that match. There were three big guys all coming into me, and I saw them coming. I just had to go through with it and I have a picture of me just going into them and punching [the ball away]. Two went down, I think, and that was *so* good. And they never came back."

Brian Glanville, one of the greatest football writers who

has ever lived in the eyes of many, once wrote a book called *Goalkeepers are Crazy* and that idea has always stayed with me since I read it as a young boy. The responsibility and the pressure that comes with being the last line of defence; surely it takes someone not sound of mind to crave that weight upon their shoulders? It is something Grodas himself has pondered and, judging by his irritated tone, had to respond to many times before.

"No, they are not crazy. Goalkeepers are brave, they are not afraid. A ski jumper is much the same. It's just something you get used to. If you are jumping 250 metres, you didn't start with that. It begins with five metres and you keep going further and further. You have to have certain personality traits to succeed in different things, and goalkeeping is the same. I see it more about this passion, this will to win. Yeah, some call it crazy. But I don't."

Grodas is a firm believer, it soon becomes apparent, in the goalkeepers' union. There's only one keeper in every team, often with several competing for one spot, and the natural human reaction, particularly in competitive sport, should be friction. In a sport that is so ruthless, goalkeeping remains a noble position.

"We're not all best friends but we respect and support and understand each other," Grodas says. "We know the situation. Goalkeeping is not easy. With this modern media and TV, everyone slaughtering goalkeepers unbearably after a mistake, it is important the goalkeepers have something in between.

"I played with a lot of goalkeepers. A lot. There are only two I really had problems working with, and I don't want to name any names. Otherwise, I really respected and wished my fellow goalkeepers well. When I coach, I want the goalkeepers to work together – if not, I take them out. I don't want goalkeepers sitting in the dressing room not talking to each other. That's bad. Goalkeepers need to discuss things, share things, give each other new thoughts. We are better than the others, I think."

Eddie Niedzwiecki played a key role in shaping Grodas's way of thinking, such was his influence as the club's goalkeeper coach. The Welshman, as mentioned previously, saw his career cruelly taken away from him through injury and denied him the opportunity to play during the traditional peak years of a goalkeeper.

Having grown up in a Norwegian football structure which was semi-professional at best until the early Nineties, it was a foreign concept for Grodas to work under a dedicated coach for his position. Niedzwiecki had done so under Peter Bonetti, who was one of the first in England to offer specialised goalkeeper training, along with Bob Wilson and Alan Hodgkinson. Armed with this experience and the requisite training, Niedzwiecki took up the trade himself and his influence can now be felt among the next generation of Norwegian goalkeepers, who Grodas now trains.

"Before him, I'd never worked with a goalkeeper coach who was at that level," he says. "He really made me understand how I could work with a structure and a meaning of doing things. He was always very prepared and put a lot of thinking behind what he was doing. There were not many goalkeepers who had this thought at the time and he was up there. As a goalkeeping coach, he was very good.

"Sometimes you meet people who really take your energy out and sometimes you feel they are average, they are not doing anything. Sometimes, very few times, you meet brilliant people who can make a difference, and Eddie was one of these people who was bringing something new. They make you think and they challenge you in a way with their thoughts and what they are doing.

"I still speak with him sometimes and he is the same good guy, very positive. He was very important in my last year at Chelsea when I didn't play. Norway had the World Cup coming up and I wanted to be part of it, and Eddie really supported me when things weren't going so well.

"Different experiences always help you, even the bad ones. I also had one year as a head coach for a Norwegian Premier League team, HamKam, after I finished playing. That was not fun. I think I got 10 years older in that year. There is something about this pressure, the media, all the negative things; so many people don't want to see you doing well. It is much easier to be a goalkeeper coach because there's not many people who really know about goalkeepers so I can just tell them to shut up! And that is *so* good."

Having criticised Gullit for the manner in which he was treated in his final months as a Chelsea player – and it is a criticism that was levelled by others, including Gavin Peacock and John Spencer, who felt they were ignored by the manager once deemed surplus to requirements – I wonder aloud if his own experience in the role has changed the way he feels about the Dutchman.

"I learned as a head coach that it's not easy to keep all the players happy," he admits. "I was a very inexperienced coach at the time, but when you are a player sat in the dressing room, you think you know everything and you have all the answers. That is not the case. For Gullit, that was the same. He didn't have any experience. I think his quality impressed me more than his work with the players. He was so calm and controlled. But I think he had something to learn with leading people.

"I was a different type of goalkeeper to what he liked – he liked more calmness, not so loud and as intense. I was not that sort of goalkeeper. The communication could have been better and it wouldn't have ended like it did. Chelsea bought De Goey and so my agent called them and asked if I was coming back after the summer. I was told to come back and fight for the place with De Goey. Fair enough. Okay. I went back but I didn't even get a number. I almost didn't get a chance to play the match part of the training every day. It was frustrating.

"Players are going to be frustrated for many reasons, but I don't think anyone deserved that treatment. It wasn't the best way of doing things. I did well in training and worked very hard, but I had no chance. Eddie did some good work and he had some hard days with me. I felt it was not right and that's why I said before that Eddie was a very important guy for me. But it's not a big case now. It's a long time ago, history – it's finished. I have fantastic respect for Gullit as a player. Maybe with Zola he is the best I ever played with."

I inform him that the little Italian was my boyhood hero and, contrary to popular belief, you should absolutely meet your hero – especially if he happens to be Gianfranco Zola, hands down the nicest man in football.

"You know, I had Pat Jennings as a coach at Tottenham, I met Ray Clemence, I worked with Packie Bonner and also met Phil Parkes at West Ham. All these legendary goalkeepers. But I missed Shilton.

"Then, in 2008, they were doing a TV programme in Norway. It was a silly show, trying to recreate all these famous episodes from the world of sport, and one of them was the

God's Hand. They were filming it in Lillestrom and Peter came to Norway to film it. I got his autograph and a picture with him. That was a big day. I have two autographs – Diego Maradona and Shilton. He was very nice."

But was he crazy?

"There are always some, we're all different. Peter and the guys I mentioned are top goalkeepers from the 1970s and '80s, and you also have in this group the Cat from Chelsea. They are all big personalities, not crazy. They are brave, not afraid."

Grodas has already given examples of what those of us raised on a diet of English football would traditionally consider brave, when he came face-to-face with the hard men of Leicester City and Wimbledon, but one moment against the former offers a far better illustration of his courage.

In all the furore surrounding the award of the late penalty, something went totally unnoticed in the moments leading up to the decision. Roberto Di Matteo had the ball on the right of midfield and, under pressure from a Leicester forward, decided to play it back to his goalkeeper. Received wisdom would suggest a big lump up field would follow, the result of which would be a 50-50 at best – perhaps even less when you consider the man-mountains playing at the back for the Foxes – and Chelsea hoping to win the second ball. Instead, Grodas took a touch and bypassed the striker bearing down on him to play a return pass to Di Matteo, who fed Eddie Newton and in turn he spun away from his marker and laid the ball off to Johnsen. What followed was the barnstorming run which resulted in the match-winning penalty. Throughout the move, there were at least four opportunities for a player to take a more direct route. That was the easy way out, but it wasn't part of Gullit's philosophy. If an example was needed of the players buying into the idea of sexy football, this was it. But they had to be brave – and Frode Grodas, the Viking warrior, certainly was.

9. Mint Moment

'Glenn Hoddle started the revolution
that set Chelsea on the road to
where the club is today, bringing
in some massive names, and
Ruud Gullit took it on.'

"On my first day of pre-season, Dmitri Kharine, who wore the No1 shirt, had to bring in biscuits – six or seven packets for the players to tuck into before training. The next day it was No2 in the squad, Stevie Clarke, then No3 and so on. When I joined I was given the No3 shirt, so on day three it was my turn. I've never been much of a biscuit man, I always preferred a bit of toast. I remember asking everyone, 'Well, what sort of biscuits should I get?' The response was typically helpful: 'Anything, just biscuits.' I think I even asked Wisey, who was the captain, just to make sure. So, I brought in these bog-standard biscuits, and he was like, 'Mints, what the heck are these! Go and get some more.' I had to drive out of the training ground to the local shop to get some more. The biscuits weren't up to standard."

It's a throwaway anecdote, but it acts as a metaphor for the football club which Scott Minto joined in 1994; aspirations to climb to the peak of the Premier League, but in reality still grounded by the spit and sawdust ways which characterised English football.

"It wasn't conducive to what Glenn Hoddle was looking to do and you could see he was perhaps frustrated by it," Minto says. "The funny thing is, it helped create a really good team spirit, but Glenn stopped it after about six months and started bringing in fruit, which was obviously far better for you. Chelsea was a club on the up, but one that needed to be changed in terms of training facilities and thinking like a big club. I signed for a club that had a great name, great tradition and a great manager. But the facilities were just shocking."

For Minto, 2017 features two big anniversaries from his football career. As well as marking two decades since Chelsea's triumph in the FA Cup final, it is 30 years since the one that got away: an FA Youth Cup final defeat with Charlton Athletic, the only time in the south London club's history that they were within touching distance of the biggest prize in English youth football.

"Do you know what that tells you?" he asks before answering his own question. "I'm getting old. And I feel it at times."

He certainly doesn't look it. At 45 years of age, Minto has retained the boyish good looks which marked him out as a Chelsea heartthrob during his three years at Stamford Bridge, and he has the charm to go with it, too. Some would say he was made for television, so it's no surprise to see him hosting Sky Sports' EFL coverage, the latest stop on a post-playing journey which began at Staffordshire University and has included stints on BBC Radio London, Revista de la Liga and Al-Jazeera, as well as our very own Chelsea TV.

Along with Frode Grodas, he is perhaps the most likely candidate to be the forgotten man of our big day out at Wembley 20 years ago, which is not intended to denigrate his contribution, rather to highlight the magnitude of the players Chelsea had managed to attract over the preceding three years. Under Hoddle we didn't only begin to think like a big club – we started to act like one, too.

Before we get on to the whys and wherefores of that change, however, some background is required on Minto's path to Chelsea and just how highly rated he was as a young footballer.

Those of you who have heard his south London accent will be surprised to learn he is from the Wirral, where he was born and spent the first three years of his life before his family relocated to Bromley, Kent. He grew up supporting Liverpool and idolising Kenny Dalglish.

"I had posters of him on my wall – he was King Kenny, he was just the man. But one day I just stopped supporting them. It wasn't a conscious thing or something I tried to do, I just naturally stopped when I joined Charlton as an apprentice.

"When it's your job, you concentrate on the team you're playing for. The reason why football is what it is, is because it's so tribal, because you're born, almost, a fan of a particular club and you stay with that club no matter what. I think that's absolutely fantastic and I'm sure if I wasn't a footballer I'd still be a Liverpool fan.

"If you ask a lot of professional footballers, they'll tell you their club has always been so and so, but if you ask them the honest truth as to how much they support them now compared to when they were growing up, it would be a lot less. I was a Liverpool fan and I stopped being a Liverpool fan at 15."

It was at that age when his football career truly took off, as Charlton made it through to the aforementioned final of the FA Youth Cup with Minto a key member of a side, and he was to receive a taster of what life in the big leagues was all about. Thankfully, he had a forgiving headmaster.

"Every time we made it through another round I'd have to ask permission from my school to have the afternoon off so I could play," Minto remembers. "It's amazing to think I was at school in the morning, doing maths, English or whatever – I think geography was the one I missed the most, that was Monday afternoon – and then travelling with the team and playing in what is the most serious competition at youth level. And at 15 years of age, I really looked it – I didn't look 17 or 18 – and you're playing against 17-year-olds who look 18 or 19.

"It was amazing, we had a really good team and we should

have won the final, but we ended up losing in extra time. What was significant about that year was who we played, because we were up against Coventry City, who had also reached the FA Cup final. It was three days before that game when we had the second leg at Highfield Road and we played in front of 17,000 people. At 15 you might as well liken that to a crowd of 90,000 when you're a professional footballer. You don't play in front of 1,000 fans, let alone 17,000, but though it was slightly surreal, it still felt natural to me and I didn't feel overawed in anyway. There were times in my career when I'd play a pre-season game or certain league matches and I'd feel really nervous. You can't put your finger on it.

"Within 18 months I was playing for the first team, which is a massive, massive jump. I don't think people quite appreciate what it takes. They watch professional footballers and they're saying, 'So and so is rubbish, he's this, that and the other.' But to actually get to that level takes a lot. To be an apprentice, you have to be a very good player. To be a reserve-team player, you have to be even better. But still, it's a massive jump to be a first-team player. And then to be a first-team player in the Premier League; well, I don't know what the maths are, but the percentage of anyone becoming one is clearly very small."

Seven years after his appearance in the Youth Cup final, Minto made the step up to the big time with Chelsea, although it should be noted he spent his first full season as a professional playing in the old Division One. The rest of his time with the Addicks was spent in the tier below, but he was capped by England at Under-21 level and, with his contract coming to an end, Arsenal and Chelsea were the two clubs vying for his signature, an indication of just how highly rated he was at that time. Highbury looked his most likely destination.

"I met up with George Graham at the end of the season," he recalls. "He told me Nigel Winterburn had waited 18 months to get into the first team before Kenny Sansom finished and I might have to do the same. I'd seen Colin Pates, who was our captain at Charlton, go to Arsenal and play in the reserves, not getting close to the first team. Patesy, obviously a Chelsea legend as well, was a really good player."

Charlton's reserve-team manager, Keith Peacock, father of then Blues midfielder Gavin, intervened and pushed Chelsea to step up their interest in the player. Peacock even helped broker the deal for Minto, effectively acting as his agent throughout the negotiations.

"I just knew I wanted to sign for Chelsea," he says. "To have the choice between them and Arsenal was amazing, really. But the chance to play for Glenn Hoddle, knowing the style of football he liked and pretty much being guaranteed first-team football, it was a no-brainer. As it happened, the first two years I kept on picking up injuries and couldn't get a run of games or a run of form.

"And if you got injured at Chelsea, my goodness it was a nightmare. The physio would have stuff for you to do every day at Stamford Bridge, so I'd have to drive from Kent round the M25, which was a nightmare anyway because of the traffic, to Harlington, and then in the afternoon I'd drive through London to get to Stamford Bridge. Then I'd drive from Stamford Bridge back to Kent, when you're getting stuck in school and then rush-hour traffic. If I was injured, which was a lot, I'd be in the car for at least three to four hours a day, which certainly isn't helpful in terms of your back or your legs. I'm sure it didn't help and I'm sure I would have been fitter if I didn't have do it, but that's hypothetical, really.

"When you're injured all the time, it's not nice at the best of times, but Glenn was fantastic with me. We had similar injuries – he'd also hurt his Achilles during his playing career – and he understood what it was like to go through that. But if anything he was too good – he was putting me in when I wasn't quite ready. I was either breaking down or not putting in the performances I knew I was capable of. It wasn't until, really, the third season that I was properly fit."

It is quite a common theme among ex-players from this generation to say Hoddle doesn't receive the credit he deserves for setting the Chelsea revolution in motion, and Minto falls into that camp. It seems strange to talk about a manager whose three years at Stamford Bridge failed to bring about a top-half finish as one of the most influential in the club's history, but his tenure in west London was about so much more than results. Having established himself as a something of a footballing demigod during his playing days, the former Spurs legend, in conjunction with the pulling power of trendy west London, allowed the Blues to attract stars well above their station. Chelsea haven't looked back since, embarking on a winning cycle which can all be traced back to that fateful summer of 1993 when David Webb was replaced by Hoddle.

While reading back on previous interviews I have conducted with Minto, I joke that our chats tend to coincide with the England manager's job being up for grabs and that he always puts Hoddle's name forward for the job. This occasion is no different; Gareth Southgate is still a few days away from being confirmed in the role full-time, but Minto feels the best option remains stuck in a pundit's chair in a television studio.

"Gareth deserves a go, but Glenn would still be my No1 choice," he insists. "It's nothing to do with how good he was as a player, because you can be a top player but not a top manager. He was a top manager. Tactically, he was the best I played under. He loved that side of things. I imagine when he was manager of England first time round that was fantastic for him because he was asking top players to do things that they can do, things that he used to be able to do. He could really form his opinions and impose them on top-class players.

"I know he's been out of the game, but he's proven; he's done the club thing, he doesn't need to go back into club management to prove he can be an England manager again. He knows the game and I definitely think it helps if you've played for your country and appeared at major tournaments. He's also managed at a World Cup. Even now, Glenn Hoddle the pundit could win over that set of players; how he talks, how he coaches. I have no doubt about that whatsoever."

One of the issues often cited with Hoddle and his subsequent lack of managerial success was his man-management skills, namely his inability to accept that the majority of players he was coaching couldn't even come close to matching his technical ability. It is a theory Minto rejects, although it was clear before Gullit and Co arrived that Hoddle was still by far and away the most skilful technician at the club.

"Technically speaking, he's the best player I ever played with," Minto says. "He could do everything with his left foot that he could with his right, and not even Zola could do that. We'd have this thing every single morning, which was to improve your technique but also to show how good Glenn was! I'm joking about that last point, but Shreevesy [Peter Shreeves, Hoddle's assistant manager] would say to us, 'Right, give me a skill.' So it would be something like: foot, thigh, head; foot, thigh, head. And everyone would have to do that. Then it would be, 'Wisey, give us another.' And he'd do outside of the left foot, shoulder, head; same again. Obviously there would be balls bouncing all over the place because some were better than others, but Glenn never dropped the ball. He was pretty much technically perfect."

The appointment of Gullit as manager sounded the death knell for the Chelsea careers of fans' favourites Gavin Peacock and John Spencer, and there was always speculation surrounding the remaining British players and their place in the set-up. The dressing room could have naturally divided – something Minto experienced to a degree later on in his career at Benfica when Graeme Souness recruited a British core – but the foundations at Chelsea were strong and the recruitment process simply solidified that, as did the relaxed environment created by the new gaffer.

"Glenn started the revolution that set Chelsea on the road to where the club is today, bringing in some massive names, and Ruud just took it on," Minto says. "Glenn was very serious, which was completely different to Ruud's approach. It was really good fun to play for him. I'm not saying it wasn't under Glenn, but Ruud wanted us to have fun, and we did. The thing about Ruud was that he brought in good characters. He didn't have to unite a dressing room because it was already close and the players he brought in weren't big-time Charlies. He didn't have to cultivate anything specifically during training. But he would come in practically every day and say, with a big smile on his face, 'Hello lovely boys. Let's have some fun.' Apparently he loved Windsor Davies and that's where it came from. And what he created was a really happy training environment.

"The changes to the playing squad were just part of the next step. Football is a ruthless game. Spenny was a character, one of the funniest guys at the club. He'd take the mickey out of Ruud even when he was manager. He was just a funny guy and the Chelsea fans loved him as well. And I got on really well with Gavin, we used to travel in together. In many ways we were two very different people, but he had a great sense of humour. In terms of the dressing room we lost two big characters, but football moves on, the dressing room moves on. There wasn't any danger to the spirit. Even if Wisey had gone, the spirit would have kept on because we just had a good group of players. Although you could tell Wisey was the captain, the gaffer in the dressing room. He was just a fantastic character. What was he, 5ft 4in? But 6ft 6in in stature. If there was anything that needed to be said, it didn't matter who you were, Wisey would certainly let people know. He ran the dressing room, really. If he felt that anyone was slacking, he'd have a go at them. He was a very, very good captain – one of the best Chelsea have had."

The end dressing room at Harlington was, during the 1996/97 season, still occupied by English players and centre-back Michael Duberry claims they called themselves The Rebels.

"We even used to call Sparky Grandad Rebel," recalls Doobs. "We got a bit of respect from the senior pros, especially the foreign ones, for the way we conducted ourselves; sometimes a bit rebellious, and they could be a bit shocked when the English culture shone through, but we had the respect of the players."

Minto does not recall the self-bestowed tag on the group, but he does remember a group of players who were far from overawed by the esteemed company they were now keeping within the football club.

"Doobs was very funny and even before he got into the first team he was the life and soul of the dressing room" he says. "He was a great character and a very good player, perhaps even one who was playing well enough to be called up for England before his injury that season. It sounds like something Doobs would say, and I wouldn't necessarily see myself as someone who was a rebel, but we were definitely in that dressing room and we definitely had a good laugh. There was me, Frank Sinclair, Andy Myers, Danny Granville was a good lad when he came in, Jody Morris and Paul Hughes. The latter was my room-mate for the Cup final.

"A group of us used to go out together regularly, but if we had official nights out with the team, everyone went. Someone like Gianfranco Zola, who didn't drink, would always come along for the first couple of hours. That's part of what made him the person he was – he was a team player. The English drinking way wasn't his style, but he still came along to everything.

"Luca Vialli, on the other hand, would stay a little bit longer. He was great fun, he loved a joke. Whenever people mention Luca, I can't help but picture this: he always used to take his kit off after training but leave his socks and boots on. So he'd be walking around naked, apart from his boots and socks! And he always had a smile on his face. He didn't know much English when he came and he had these kiddies books that he'd read out loud. Wisey used to take the mickey out of him, but he was a great character, a great laugh."

After two years filled with injury setbacks, the new arrivals coincided with Minto getting himself fully fit and enjoying his best season with the club. He played regularly on the left-hand side of Gullit's favoured 3-5-2 formation and found a manager who understood more than just his strengths as a footballer, but readily accepted his limitations as a wing-back. Nowadays, the role requires the ultimate athlete, someone who is always in a position to offer his team an option in the attacking third but without compromising his defensive duties. The distance covered by Marcos Alonso and Victor Moses, the two wing-backs for Chelsea during the 2016/17 season under Antonio Conte, reflects that change. Twenty years earlier, there was less emphasis on athleticism.

"Ruud understood the wing-back role. Dan Petrescu was the ultimate model for the position in that era, and what a player he was, by the way. Technically brilliant, very clever, not the quickest but quick when he needed to be and even sharper in the mind. He wasn't the strongest of defenders, so the wing-back role suited him, because he had Duberry behind him who would just mop up everything and no one would beat him for pace or strength. Ruud knew that in the wing-back role against a 4-4-2, which most teams used in those days, you can't continually be taking on their full-back and defending against their winger. Otherwise you might as well get Linford Christie or some distance runner in to do that. I played in the position later on at West Ham and Trevor Sinclair was on the other side, a fantastic athlete who could get up and down for 90 minutes and then say, 'Right, shall we do another 90 minutes.' I wasn't. I had to time my runs and in that sense I was a bit like Dan – not the ultimate athlete, but clever enough to pick and choose my runs and make them at the right time.

"Without a doubt, by letting me play my game and under-standing there are certain things you can and can't do in that wing-back role, it got me to the season I had and the goals I scored, because I was able to get myself into some very good positions going forward."

After an injury-plagued couple of years at the Bridge, Minto was determined to keep his place in the side, even if that meant playing through the pain barrier as he struggled to overcome his Achilles issues.

"If you ask any footballer, you always have niggles and stuff going into games," he says. "There was a game against Man United, when Zola scored that wonderful solo goal, and I couldn't even run in the warm-up. But I didn't want to say that I wasn't right. Even in the first 10 minutes, if David Beckham had pushed the ball past me I wouldn't have been able to run. You sort of position yourself in a way to not let him do that, and then it warms up and you end up having a decent game. There were a lot of times in that last season when I wasn't 100 per cent fit, but you just play through it

"There were times when it was almost as if it was a kiss of death being a left-back at Chelsea. I knew about the problems they'd had before I signed and I felt I was getting it while I was there. I'm not a superstitious person, but I felt the No3 shirt was bad luck for me so I changed to 17 for my third season. It's hard as a professional footballer when you get injured and you keep on getting injured. You look at different things. You put pressure on yourself to perform and to do everything right and when it's not happening you beat yourself up about it. It wasn't until that third season that I wasn't just showing it in games here and there; I'm fit, I know I can show what I can do."

It ended with Minto taking his place in the side for the FA Cup final against Middlesbrough. The rediscovered confidence shone through.

"Considering it was the biggest game of my career, I was fine in the build-up to the game," he remembers. "Even though the FA Cup has lost a bit of its glamour and gloss, I'm very much a traditionalist and I think the FA Cup is very important in this country. I was brought up in the Seventies, where the whole day was taken up by the FA Cup final. You'd get Blankety Blank between the finalists' fans, all kinds of different shows to build up to the final. For me, the FA Cup was absolutely massive and I knew there would be millions of people around the world watching it, as well as 80,000 in the stadium. Yet I felt surprisingly calm. I remember listening to this song, the name of which escapes me but it was some sort of house tune, and it just had the right balance between getting me going and keeping me relaxed. It got to about 2.40pm and I was still listening to this song, and Ruud said, 'Don't you think you should start thinking about the game now?' But I was just thinking, 'I know what's out there, I know what I'm up against. I want to keep my mind as positive as possible.'

"I just felt really good. Even walking out the tunnel, I could feel it was an iconic moment, but also I was of a mindset, because the season had gone so well, that this was just another game and we were going to win this. As a one-off game, that's the best moment of my career, without a doubt."

The FA Cup final was Minto's last game for Chelsea. The club which had taken full advantage of the Bosman rule was now on the receiving end, losing its left wing-back to Benfica, where a foreign invasion of its own was taking place. Instead of Italians, the club turned its attention to Brits; Minto was the first to arrive, soon to be followed by manager Graeme Souness and players Brian Deane, Michael Thomas, Dean Saunders, Mark Pembridge, Steve Harkness and Gary Charles. Though the experiment failed to bring about the same level of success enjoyed by Chelsea, Minto rates the experience among his career highlights.

"When my contract was coming to an end, Kenny Dalglish tried to buy me for Newcastle. I told him he was my hero when I was growing up and he had a laugh, but I'd decided to make a lifestyle change as well as a club change. If I was going to leave Chelsea, it was going to be for something special. And to go to a club like Benfica and live that foreign lifestyle, experience a different culture and language, was definitely something special. Otherwise I wouldn't have left Chelsea. I was happy, but at the same time I just saw Chelsea going down a foreign route, which was actually very successful, and even though that last season was arguably my best ever, I still feel my biggest achievement was doing really well at Benfica. I absolutely loved my time there. It was so different from what you experience in England. There were 5,000 people watching my first day of pre-season training, which brought home the size and stature of the club, and we had 80,000 for a pre-season game against Lazio when they unveiled all the new signings.

"I lived in Cascais, which was 20 minutes from Lisbon, and it was right on the Atlantic Ocean. I'd wake up and look out at the ocean – it was wonderful. The food was incredible, fresh fish caught that day. You'd drive down the little roads by the coast in the middle of January and still have your windows down, it was still lovely and warm. You could eat outside all year around. It was the perfect lifestyle for me, I loved it. It was great on and off the pitch.

"We qualified for the Champions League and I played in four of the six games – I was out injured for the other two – but the format was different in those days so not all second-placed sides went through, which meant we were eliminated at the group stage. Lining up while they played the Champions League anthem is something I'll never forget. Although I did score what was then the quickest own goal in the competition's history! It was at the Estadio da Luz against Helsinki. We went 2-1 up after that, but ended up drawing 2-2. I didn't feel too bad about the own goal because, it was very harsh to give it to me anyway, but the next day we went for a warm down and there were a few hundred Benfica fans who came along and they were cheering my name to try to make me feel better. That was really nice of them, a lovely gesture which shows what sort of relationship I had with the fans."

He returned to England after 18 months to join West Ham, and one of my final memories of Minto the footballer comes from his time with the Hammers. In March 2002, armed with the knowledge that Zola had been selected for Chelsea's reserve side for a match against West Ham United, my father and I travelled to Aldershot Town for another opportunity to see the Italian maestro in action, worried it might for the last time with rumours abound that his time with Chelsea was coming to an end. If memory serves, he scored an outstanding goal that Monday evening, possibly from a free-kick, but it was another incident from the match which stayed with me. It involved Minto steaming into a challenge which wiped out Gianfranco, prompting as angry a response as I've ever seen from the most genial of footballers. If that was completely out of character, what followed was perfectly in keeping with the man we all know and love.

"I remember that, and I find it funny that you do as well! Why he was in reserves I have no idea, but we had a little chat and a hug in the tunnel before the game. I like to think

I wasn't a dirty player, so shall we say I mistimed the tackle? I was half a yard off the pace, I was just back from another injury. I remember him getting up to have a go, which he didn't do very often in his career, and he wasn't happy at all. I don't know if that had anything to do with him playing in the first place... Then he looked at me as if to say, 'Oh, it's you,' and he gave me a hug! It summed him up perfectly. What a top man.

"I saw him a few years ago at a charity event and I asked him if he would appear on a show I was doing for Al-Jazeera. When I told them he'd said yes, they thought it was amazing and decided to make the whole show about him, but then it transpired he was playing golf in Wentworth with this guy from Italy who he hadn't seen in years, and we weren't quite sure if he'd get back in time. Al-Jazeera wanted to send a car to get him, but going through the London traffic would be a nightmare. 'Don't worry, Scott, I'll just get the train,' he told me.

"You've got Gianfranco, still in his golf gear and with all his clubs, travelling on the train to Waterloo, and we're still not sure he's going to make it so Nigel Spackman, funnily enough, was booked as a stand-in. Gianfranco turned up half an hour before we went on air, got changed and we did a brilliant show with him. Most people, especially someone as legendary as him, would have just cancelled and said they couldn't make it. But he didn't want to do that. That's Gianfranco."

GIANFRANCO
ZOLA

10. Little Magician

'Everything came together like magic.
I was in a state of mind where I was
just playing freely. Focused but free.
The Chelsea fans sing *Carefree* and
for me that is how it felt.'

"It was a good pass from Roberto Di Matteo. I was running from the middle of the area towards the left and then I decided to change direction suddenly with a backheel. It put me in a good position to score. The defender didn't expect me to change so quickly and I surprised him."

Gianfranco Zola is sat in the upper tier of the East Stand at Stamford Bridge and he is putting a few of his greatest goals for the Blues into words at the behest of Chelsea TV and William Hill, starting with his famous effort against Wimbledon in the 1997 FA Cup semi-final, when it felt as if he had frozen every other player in time for just one second. It's almost a pointless exercise; just like asking Mozart to talk you through one of his symphonies step by step, the words will never come close to matching the sheer wonderment inspired by the real thing.

The goals are being shown on the big screen which straddles the East Stand and the Shed End, and in between takes Zola rubs his hands together and blows on his fingers. It is exactly the type of day which makes me wonder what he sees in London when he could be back home in sunny Sardinia, for the biting wind cuts through the stadium and all he has protecting the top half of his body is a William Hill polo shirt. But throughout the half an hour he spends going over goal after goal, there is not one word of complaint. Even requests to repeat a take are not met with any dissent, just a polite smile and complete professionalism. Move on to the next one.

"This goal was very spectacular. Graeme [Le Saux] took the corner very low, I thought it would be higher for me to head, so in this moment I had to invent something. I tried this backflick many times but I never managed to get it right, but fortunately that day it came off quite well. At the time, I didn't realise how I scored. I had wanted to do that, but it happened so quickly I didn't realise what I did. I only saw it later when I watched it on TV. The players were so amazed and I didn't know why! When I saw it on TV later on I realised it was quite a nice goal."

As you may have already guessed, he is describing his goal against Norwich City, which prompted a eureka moment within Stamford Bridge. Like the Italian, most people inside the stadium had no idea quite what we had just witnessed, for it all happened in the blink of an eye within a mass of bodies inside the penalty box. The replay appeared on the big screen and a few thousand figured out what had happened. The collective "wow" could be heard above the ripple of applause, prompting the next replay of the goal to be viewed in near silence. Then it hit us. Clarity. The response was a mixture of astonishment and admiration. Even as he approached the autumn of a Chelsea career filled with moments of sheer brilliance, he still had the capacity to amaze us.

"The pleasure of scoring goals for this club is something that remains unique for me," he tells the camera, wrapping up his filming session in the stands. "It's special for me to have this connection with this great club and these great people and supporters."

The main purpose of his return to his spiritual home is to partake in a question and answer session with a group of journalists and the former Blues centre-half Paul Elliott, a man Zola would almost certainly have called a team-mate had injury not cruelly robbed him of his career in the nascent days of the Premier League. It's a long day. He arrived early in the afternoon and has other business to attend to in London before the Q&A will eat into most of his evening, but he has promised me an hour of his time before he takes to the stage, and one thing you can be sure of with this affable fellow is that he will be true to his word. Even Roman Abramovich, in the days following his purchase of Chelsea, discovered that to his cost when he realised there was simply no way of convincing Zola to break his promise to join Cagliari, the Sardinian club so dear to his heart.

We meet in the Copthorne Hotel at Stamford Bridge, accompanied by Chelsea's player liaison officer Gary Staker, whose fluent grasp of Italian bridged the language barrier and helped establish a close friendship with Zola from the first day he arrived at the club. They have remained firm friends ever since, the bond established over the construction of Ikea flatpack furniture the night before his home debut against Newcastle United.

"In his first three days at Harlington the training was electric," reported the matchday programme ahead of that game. "His ability to beat people and open up play had everyone stepping up a gear."

Midfielder Gavin Peacock, who had fallen out of the first-team reckoning and was soon to be heading across west London to sign for Queens Park Rangers, remembers it well.

"I was buzzing that we'd signed him and it was the same around the training ground," recalls the man whose brace sent us through to the FA Cup final in 1994. "I was in the team against him and, as you may recall, I wasn't a tackler but I thought I would nail him anyway! The ball was played to him, I've slid in and then his quick feet have got him past me and he's gone. 'Wow, he's lively,' I thought to myself.

"After about 20 minutes, someone managed to do a better job than me and so his team had a free-kick about 25 yards from goal. He put the ball down and then Ruud said something to him in Italian. He stepped back, whipped the ball over the wall and into the top corner. Everyone gave him a round of applause – whoever you are, to do that on your first day at training and make that sort of impression was very good.

"But then Gullit stopped us, we didn't play on, and he got Zola to place the free-kick again. Kevin Hitchcock lined up his wall and he knew where it was going: over the wall and into the top corner. But there was still nothing he could do about it. Zola must have taken six free-kicks and got four or five in. Remarkable. What a level of skill."

As impressive as the club's recruitment had been, and a far cry from earlier in the decade when there were far more misses than hits, the team which went on to establish themselves as Chelsea greats would not have done so without Zola. Yes, there was some degree of flair, but it was largely to be found at the back, from Frank Leboeuf, or from Dan Petrescu out wide and on those rare occasions when Gullit's weary limbs allowed him to pull on the boots and turn back the years. Then it all changed. Fantasy. Zola brought the best out in everyone, which is the mark of a great player.

His arrival, coming just a couple of weeks after vice-chairman Matthew Harding lost his life in a helicopter crash, was a ray of sunshine just when the club needed it most.

If Gullit had made it look, in the words of Hoddle, like he was an 18-year-old playing in a game of Under-12s, Zola was playing football from elsewhere in the galaxy. It was as if he was showing us a new sport. In just his sixth game as a Blue, against West Ham United, he came up against notorious hardman Julian Dicks and scored a goal which had us shaking our heads in disbelief. Running at pace, he turned the burly defender one way, then the other, and back again, before firing a crisp shot into the far corner. On the same day, Eric Cantona scored his famous chip against Sunderland, celebrated so nonchalantly. The beautiful game was suddenly once again an apt moniker for our sport – and Chelsea Football Club would never be the same again.

To think we nearly missed out on all that magic. Three weeks before he signed for the Blues, Zola had been touted around to other clubs, including one just up the road; Spurs had the opportunity to sign a player who would become recognised as one of the greatest in our history. Instead, Zola's arrival on these shores was met with a rant from Alan Sugar, who was then chairman of Tottenham Hotspur, about "soccer's foreign mercenaries". The north London side had been given an all-too-fleeting glimpse of the galvanising effect of an overseas star after Jurgen Klinsmann wooed White Hart Lane, winning the Football Writers' Association player of the year award at the end of his first season with the club, only to depart soon after for Bayern Munich.

"I forecast that by May 1997 many of these foreign legion, the famous people at certain clubs, will not be coming back to England," he said. "They're only here for a year to better themselves for their own personal gain."

In fact, May 1997 was the month in which Chelsea lifted the FA Cup for the first time in 27 years, shortly after Zola had followed Klinsmann and Cantona in winning the FWA award. He was the best player in the top flight, which at the time also begged the question of when, if ever, could Chelsea have claimed to have the very best in England?

That it arrived six months after Zola's arrival, which is now considered to be the minimum bedding-in period of a player from overseas, made it all the remarkable. Along with received wisdom that he was too small and too weak to adapt to the physical demands of English football, Zola had well and truly ripped up the rulebook.

"I think it was a combination of things that allowed me to do that," he explains. "Firstly, I had a great desire to do well in my experience in England, and I had a fantastic team to play in. They supported me very much – my success at Chelsea could only be possible with the players alongside me. Also, I adapted my qualities to English football and I made it very effective for the style over here. So all of these factors contributed to that award."

Brilliantly, this "foreign mercenary" was a man so modest his own father only found out he won the Footballer of the Year honour by reading about it in the newspaper. Ignacio Zola promptly made his first trip to England to see his son receive the distinguished award from none other than Sir Stanley Matthews, the original 'Wizard of the Dribble'.

"I like watching him, he's such an entertaining little fellow," said Matthews, the first-ever winner of the prize and surely a better judge of footballer than Sugar.

As Gullit prepared to whisk his pocket rocket away from the ceremony and into a cab, he lost sight of him. Where had he gone? To shake the hand of everyone sat at the top table. It was a scene which played out in similar fashion 18 years later, when he attended the ceremony to accept the award on behalf of Eden Hazard, who was unable to collect his award due to the removal of his wisdom teeth earlier that day.

More success followed in Zola's second season, which culminated in a moment destined to be replayed again and again in the years which followed.

The European Cup Winners' Cup final of 1998 gave the

club its second opportunity to lift the trophy, having beaten Real Madrid in 1971, but a drab game in Stockholm against VfB Stuttgart was in danger of heading into extra time until the arrival from the substitutes' bench of the little Italian.

"Twenty seconds, maybe 22," is his estimation for how long he'd spent on the pitch before his thumping finish. "Only three touches – one to control with the left, then I tried to take the man on but he stopped me, then the finish after a great pass by Dennis. I didn't wait for the ball to lift, I really hit it at the right moment in the right spot and that's why it flew so well."

The celebration was as explosive as the finish, an outpouring of emotion which was not in keeping with the happy-go-lucky chap we had become accustomed to.

"Emotionally, there was a lot going on. Firstly, there was the thought I couldn't play this game. I tore my hamstring against Liverpool and normally you don't play after 20 days with this injury, it should be more than a month. Secondly, I made it in time for that and then I wasn't starting. I came on quite late in the game. There was a lot of things going on, but sometimes as a footballer you need this. You get upset and it gives you energy, a kick up the backside as you might say. Sometimes I felt I needed to be upset, to show something to anyone, to give me extra strength and energy."

That mentality was sculpted in Sardinia, where he was born in the village of Oliena, two hours from the capital of Cagliari and a place where the olive trees are plentiful but professional footballers not so. It was a long, arduous journey to the top of the football ladder.

Luciano Moggi is known in Italy largely for his role in the Calciopoli match-fixing scandal which came to light in 2006, shortly before the Azzurri defied the odds to win their fourth

World Cup. At the time he had been working for Juventus, but before that he was employed by Napoli and he was the first top-level sporting director in Italy to take a punt on a talented young player, bringing Zola to the club as the understudy to the great Diego Maradona. He was 23 at the time and there was a real danger he could have flown under the radar, a pleasure only to be enjoyed by those on the island of Sardinia.

"I'm from a small village, only 9,000 people living there, where there were lots of outdoor activities to do, but mainly football, fishing, which I was a little bit into, and hunting," Zola says. "It was basically football, football, football for me. As you know, I was quite small until I was... now! So there were always a lot of question marks about me: 'Yes, that guy is very good. He's fast, technically he's very good. But he's small. I'm not sure, I think he's too small for the big leagues.' That was the thing. I started to catch attention when I played for the equivalent of a League Two team, Sassari Torres, where I proved that even if I wasn't that tall I could still make a difference."

He flourished in Naples, eventually replacing the world's greatest player, who he learned so much from, and moved to Parma to enhance his career prospects further. If Blues fans have plenty to thank Carlo Ancelotti for after he was at the helm of the first Chelsea side to win the domestic Double, we have even more to be appreciative of when you consider his role in Zola's move to the capital. Then a rookie manager, he saw fit to utilise the playmaker on the right-hand side of midfield amidst an abundance of attacking options. Unhappy at his perceived demotion and frustrated by the shackles placed on footballers in Italy, both on and off the pitch, Zola sought a new adventure abroad.

Where Chelsea and Glenn Hoddle had failed the previous year to prise him away from the Stadio Tardini, frightened off by a £10 million price tag, a disappointing start to a season – which had followed a disastrous Euro '96 for Zola and the Azzurri – offered the Blues a second chance.

What did he expect to happen when he joined Chelsea?

"It was very simple: I just wanted to do well and to enjoy my football," Zola responds. "If I enjoy something and do it with a smile on my face, things happen."

Zola's joie de vivre wasn't to everyone's liking, though, least of all Sir Alex Ferguson. His Manchester United side were on the receiving end of this smiling assassin on several occasions, including one jinking run and cheeky finish in his first season. The manager's respect was begrudging.

"He was always one of those players who was unperturbed about who he was playing against," he once said. "You always saw a smile on his face, and that annoyed me. How can be enjoying himself playing against United? Nobody else does."

But enjoy himself he did. After seven years of playing in Serie A, Zola felt ready for a change, and the Premier League offered him the perfect stage to shine.

"I enjoyed Italy very much and if it wasn't the way it was there I probably would never have become the player that I was," he says. "But I came to a stage where I probably needed a little more fun. Not only all the time pressure, pressure, pressure. In that sense, England was perfect. It was a very high, competitive league and at the same time players used to have a lot of fun. This was one of the reasons I really liked and enjoyed it.

"In Italy, football was huge, everything was taken to an extreme; every aspect of the game was looked after and in my opinion I think it was too much. When I came here I found a high level of football but above all else enjoyment. I appreciated that very much and that's one of the reasons myself and many others played for so long for this wonderful club and played great football for such a long time.

"There were a lot of very good things in Italy: the preparation, the attention to detail when it came to food, rest, everything. But it was also very, very intense. It was getting to an extreme where you couldn't laugh before a match, you couldn't go for a walk in the city centre, it was very stressful. So when I came over here it was like going back in time when I played football for fun. I enjoyed that.

"Everything came together like magic. I was playing in a state of mind where I was just playing freely. Focused but free. The Chelsea fans sing *Carefree* and for me that is how it felt. And it was an opportunity to have a life outside the game. I could walk down the street and be myself, not just Gianfranco Zola the footballer. It was good for me."

Even now, in an age when selfies and social media reign supreme, a hotel bar teeming with Chelsea supporters awaiting the presence of their hero on stage is filled with respectfulness. Only occasionally is our interview interrupted for a quick photo, each of which is politely requested and followed by a warm thank you, a sentiment reciprocated by Zola, who feels genuine affection towards the fans of this football club.

"I could not have expected even in my wildest dreams to enjoy such a special relationship with the supporters," he says. "I remember their *One Mrs Zola* chant after I signed a new contract one year and it really made me smile. This relationship is one of the things that surprised me the most, it was absolutely unbelievable but such a wonderful thing.

"We, as players, felt the excitement that the supporters had. That is why we are still coming back here and we get goosebumps when we speak about it. We all felt something good about it. Chelsea was coming up as a team and we were enjoying it. That could be felt by the players on the pitch."

The influence Zola had on team-mates, whether veterans or relative novices, was equally telling. A so-called skills circuit was put on for the players after training, a session which largely consisted of the young English players in the squad honing different techniques and working at improving their weaker foot. As much as it was for their benefit, it's only human instinct to see extra training as a form of punishment. One day, a little maestro with all of the tricks of the trade, proficient with either foot, rocked up at the session to join these youngsters. All of a sudden, it went from punishment to pleasure, and they learned the best lesson you can teach a footballer – no matter how good you are, practice always make perfect.

The proof of the pudding is in the eating: 14 of his 80 goals for the club came direct from free-kicks. And don't underestimate the impact his attitude had on two future legends of this football club, Frank Lampard and John Terry. The latter's ability on his left side developed to such an extent that his long-distance passing with his so-called weaker foot became pin-point and arguably more accurate than with his right. Lampard, too, was able to strike the ball cleanly with either foot and he honed a method of free-kick taking which became a valuable source of goals to him. Both Chelsea legends have spoken highly of the influence of Zola on the training ground.

"It's great to hear that and you are always pleased if ever someone speaks highly of you," Zola says. "But everything they achieved is down to them. I could be the most inspirational person in the world, but if you don't have the qualities like they have, and work hard on them, you won't achieve everything they have. And they have definitely achieved a lot – congratulations to both of them for all they have done for Chelsea.

"I'm very proud to say we helped them, not only myself but Roberto Di Matteo, Frank Leboeuf, Marcel Desailly, Gus Poyet and others. They gave to the players another way to play football, another level. I think it was good because many picked it up and they found it very beneficial.

"I should also say I did that extra work because I always liked it, not just to help the younger players. It is exactly the same as golf – I love to play the game, but I also like to go and practice it. That's part of it. Skills are not born within you, they are acquired through exercise, through practice. For some it's hard work, for others it is enjoyment. That's the reason I improved so much in certain ways. I practised joyfully all the time and things became natural to me."

The added level of professionalism is a big part of the legacy of the foreign invasion, not only at Chelsea but across the country. It has not, however, resulted in an upturn in the fortunes of the national side, who have been unable to pass the quarter-finals of a major tournament in the 20 years that followed Zola's arrival on these shores. He, like the rest of us, remains baffled by that.

"I cannot believe what happened at the Euros," he says of England's exit at the hands of Iceland. "I thought they were going to do well at the World Cup in Brazil, but I knew they were young and they could have some problems. But in the Euros, I was surprised. I expected more. It's something that interests me, how the players cannot maintain the same level when they play games in the national team. Pity, because this England team has got potential."

Zola remained at Chelsea until the summer of 2003, having played 311 games, a club record at the time for most appearances by an overseas player. His tally of 80 goals doesn't tell the full story of his influence, as he was as much a creator as he was a scorer, and his wizardry with the ball at his feet left fans gasping in disbelief.

His final act as a player at Chelsea was to run rings around Jamie Carragher by the corner flag, leaving the defender on his backside and swiping aimlessly at thin air, as full-time edged ever closer in a game against Liverpool which would confirm our place back amongst Europe's elite at the expense of the Reds. It felt as if he was giving us one final moment to remember him by, the exclamation mark at the end of an extraordinary seven years.

That season culminated with him picking up the Chelsea Player of the Year award for the second time, which is all the more impressive when you consider he had spent much of the previous season on the bench and seemingly heading for a damp squib of an exit. We should have known he would have one last trick up his sleeve.

"That was my miracle, if I can say that. I didn't play much the previous year and people were saying that I was finished. I remember speaking to the manager at the end of that season and telling him, 'Next year I'm going to come back stronger than ever.' I worked hard all through the summer and when I came back I was sharp and I was focused. Things went really well and I rate that as one of my best years, if not the best."

As exciting as the arrival of Abramovich was that summer,

it was tinged with sadness when a day later it was confirmed Zola would be leaving these shores to play for his hometown club. He had given his word to Cagliari before the takeover was complete and it was the toughest decision of his career.

"It was very, very difficult for me," Zola explains. "Cagliari were looking for an answer and I knew I had to make a move. Chelsea were having financial problems, but it wasn't the main reason. I think I finished on a high and I wanted to leave the place like that. I also wanted to finish my career in Sardinia in Cagliari. It was a good opportunity. They were the main reasons, but I can assure you it was very tough. Especially after I made the decision. Then I found myself in quite a difficult situation. I think he tried to buy me back from Cagliari. I've got to say, Roman was good – he tried very hard to bring me back, first as a footballer and then in another capacity. I'm really thankful for that. But I don't regret anything. I had a fantastic time at Chelsea but it was my dream to one day go back to Sardinia and play one or two years for my team there."

If anything, it simply made the supporters love him even more. We adored him for his skills on the pitch, but he was just as admired for his qualities as a human being. If he had gone back on his word to Cagliari, the legacy he'd written for himself would have become a myth.

"Exactly. Trust me, it didn't come easily to make that decision, but once I took it I didn't want to change my mind. It was amazing to see all the Chelsea fans who came out to watch Cagliari games when I was there and I tried to make sure I cuddled all of them because it meant so much to me! I felt so privileged to have these people come to see me and I really enjoyed it."

A year later, he was offered the chance to say a proper goodbye to the supporters with a farewell match against Real Zaragoza. As he departed the scene of his second home for the last time, Zola thanked everyone for giving him this opportunity. There was no need. He had given us more than we could have ever dreamed of.

11. Luca

'I think the pillars were already there,
but we finished building the first, second
and third floor. Then there was a bit of
a gap, but Roman arrived and they
made a skyscraper.'

"Ruud was shocked, I believe, when he was sacked, just as I was when it happened to me a couple of years later. We didn't have a chance to talk after he left. Actually, I think we made an effort to avoid seeing each other, even in public places. Then, when I was sacked, Ruud said something like, 'What goes around comes around,' which I didn't like as a comment. I thought it was unfair and unnecessary.

"I think 10 years, probably even longer, had passed by without us seeing each other when I went over to Bahrain to play in a Pro-Am golf event. I went down for breakfast, got my stuff, turned around and saw there was only a table for two available – and there was Ruud, sat on the opposite side of it! So I sat down at his table, and we talked..."

In my head, I'm imagining events in this plush hotel in the Persian Gulf unfolding like one of the great moments in cinematic history, the scene played out between two icons of the silver screen, Robert De Niro and Al Pacino, in Michael Mann's crime thriller *Heat*. This time it was two footballing greats coming face-to-face for the first time since the saga which saw one of them ousted as manager, replaced at the helm by the player he had convinced to join him at the football club; allegations of back-stabbing in the air, a chance to settle this once and for all.

"But we didn't talk about *that!*"

Gianluca Vialli flashes that familiar grin of his. Life is too short to bear grudges, especially when you've enjoyed a hugely successful career as a footballer and, briefly, as a manager and are now paid to watch the beautiful game and educate the masses with your opinion. That he does this almost exclusively for Sky Italia is a loss to the British football-watching public, many of whom were wooed by his knowledge and charm during his appearances for the BBC during Euro 2016. Then again, if they employed him on a more regular basis there is a chance he'd have to share the stage with Gullit, and perhaps the scene from *Heat* would become more than just a figment of my imagination. Or not. Whatever problems occurred between two of the biggest personalities in the history of Chelsea Football Club are firmly in the past.

Indeed, Vialli remains grateful his old manager convinced him to come to west London in the first place. He has remained here ever since, racking up the air miles on his weekly commute to Italy, and he lives close enough to "hear the roar of the supporters" at Stamford Bridge when the ball hits the back of the net, although the wind has to be blowing in the right direction. It's a sound he became increasingly familiar with during four years at the club. To those who say Vialli failed to live up to his billing as a player for Chelsea, the Italian can point to a scoring ratio of just shy of a goal every other game, a statistic made all the more impressive by the sporadic opportunities he was afforded in his first season and combining playing and managerial duties for the best part of 18 months.

When Gullit took the reins at Chelsea in 1996, the fans had hoped his serious connections, matched by his reputation, would mean he was able to attract the big names to west London. They didn't come much bigger than Vialli, a player who was lauded in his homeland for helping Sampdoria win their first Scudetto, a season in which he finished as Serie A's top scorer, and then winning the Champions League at Juventus after the club had paid a world-record transfer fee to sign him.

His next move would come just days after he had lifted the

trophy as captain of the Bianconeri and he wouldn't cost the Blues a penny.

"The Bosman rule made your life as a professional footballer so much easier," Vialli says. "No transaction involved, your current club didn't even have to speak to anyone, it was just you and the club you wanted to join. So, it was a major opportunity for a guy like me who wanted to play away from Italy. I wouldn't necessarily call it the start of player power, but there were definitely more opportunities to mastermind your own future.

"Signing players like that was part of the new philosophy at Chelsea. It was a club that was happy to get players from the continent with the minimum transfer fee required but a good salary. And everyone at that time wanted to come to the Premiership, to come to London and to play for Chelsea. But it nearly didn't happen.

"I never had an agent in my life, but because I was so focused on trying to win the Champions League with Juventus, I asked a guy to work for me for four months. As I said, the Premiership really interested me and so did London. I spoke to David Platt, who I'd played with in Italy and who was now playing for Arsenal, but he said the manager at the time, Bruce Rioch, was only interested in British players. Then my guy spoke to Glenn Hoddle, who was still manager of Chelsea, but he wanted a younger player. Glasgow Rangers were extremely keen and I got as far as talking about money with them. I'd already met Walter Smith and the chairman, David Murray. They were incredibly wealthy and very enthusiastic about signing me.

"Then Ruud became Chelsea manager. I knew him because we'd spent some time together on holiday with our families and we played against each other many times in Italy. He called me and said, 'Luca, would you like to join me at Chelsea?' Of course!"

A general rule of thumb when it comes to fashion is that the most stylish man in the room is always the Italian. Today is no different and it is appropriate that Vialli's earliest memories of Chelsea centre on two pieces of attire.

"I think I was about 10 when my neighbour, who was one of my best friends, had been in England and he came back with a Chelsea scarf. That was the first time I heard about the club. Then, when I was in my early twenties and playing for Sampdoria, I was quite keen on different football shirts. A friend of mine went to London and he got me a bomber jacket of Chelsea, Tottenham and another club I don't remember. Sometimes I would even go to the Sampdoria training ground wearing my Chelsea jacket. I've been trying to find the picture of me wearing this, the fans would have gone mad for it! Unfortunately, I've never been able to find it."

He knew if he was to make a success of himself in England, the language barrier would have to be overcome, and it is a credit to Vialli that he picked it up relatively quickly. One of the things which always interested me about him was his use of the language. In his first interview with the matchday programme, he claimed he made the transfer after "Chelsea twisted my arm" and Mark Hughes has already explained how the Italian's early months at the club were spent pinning useful phrases to the wall of the dressing room. His interviews were always littered with English idioms, which endeared him ever more to the Chelsea supporters, but there was a purpose beyond merely sounding like your average footballer.

"I had a book when I first came to England to learn the

language, and there was a chapter about how you would say Italian cliches in English, because the literal translation wouldn't always work," Vialli explains. "I learned them all: work your socks off, fit as a fiddle, game of two halves, over the moon. The one everyone remembers was the mistake I made during a press conference when I said, 'When the fish are down.' In Italy we say fiches, which is the French way of saying chips. But obviously it sounds like fish. So I used this word by mistake, everybody laughed, but it was fine – as long as I got my message across. Sometimes you can use five words which sums up something you otherwise have to say with 1,000. Now, I kind of hate cliches, but back then I thought they were useful."

Being able to speak English – "so I can meet people, travel the world, do everything I want in my life" – was a big attraction to come to Chelsea but one incident in particular made Vialli realise how much he had to learn.

"On my first pre-season we were somewhere in Cornwall and I went to watch a movie with Dennis Wise and some of the other guys," he recalls. "It was *The Rock,* with Sean Connery and Nicolas Cage. I thought I kind of knew English a little bit, because in Italy you learned the basics: what's your name, what's your job, the book is on the table or how can I get there. The kind of stuff that is perfect for tourists. So I watched the movie and in two hours the only thing I understood was when Sean Connery was offered a coffee and he said 'no thank you'. That was the only thing I understood! That made me extremely worried. Then I listened to Dennis and that got me even more worried, because I thought I was never going to be able to speak like that!

"But I had people like Terry Byrne, David Lee and Kevin

Hitchcock, and they could see I was really making an effort, I was serious, so they gave me a hand. It was probably quite funny for some of the players, but I was dedicated to learn the language as quickly and as well as possible.

"It actually helped me when Roberto and Gianfranco joined the club, because you're in this together and not by yourself. They were willing to learn the language as much as I was, so we were making an effort to speak English whenever we were at the training ground, on the bus, at the hotel. It's just manners. I'm in your country with you, we're in the dressing room and I'm not going to speak Italian. It's about respect."

Fitting in off the pitch proved to be a doddle in comparison with events on it, where Vialli struggled for form throughout his early months. Though he was chipping in with goals, he was not affecting games in the manner he had become accustomed to and his fitness was also becoming an issue as the rigours of the English game took their toll. His relationship with Gullit became strained as a result of this and the signing of Gianfranco Zola and his subsequent pairing with Mark Hughes left Vialli as the elephant in the room. How could it have come to this at Chelsea? The Premier League era had begun with a strike pairing of Robert Fleck and Mick Harford. Now there wasn't room to accommodate a European Cup winner up front.

"Franco and Sparky were like a marriage made in heaven, they were made to play together and hit it off straight away," Vialli says. "I realised Ruud had lost a lot of confidence in my ability to play for the team. At that time I think he was probably wishing I wasn't around now that he'd found this great partnership. While I understand that a manager has to pick whoever he thinks is right for the team, I didn't like the way he treated me. I thought it would be different because of our relationship in the past, my age and how I'd played in the past. Players talk about respect, and that doesn't necessarily mean to pick someone in the team – but at least talk to him. Don't say he is a jinx when the press ask why you're not playing him. He was basically saying every time I play the side loses. Our relationship at one point was barely a professional one. It was difficult."

It was at this time that another of those iconic Chelsea moments occurred. During a game at Derby County, with Vialli once again consigned to the substitutes' bench, Dennis Wise found the back of the net and headed towards the touchline where his unhappy team-mate was sitting. He pulled up his shirt to reveal a message: "Cheer up Luca. We love you XXX."

"I had no idea whatsoever he was planning this," Vialli says. "In fact, when I saw it my first thought was, 'What does cheer up mean'! It wasn't on my wall, you see. I knew what 'cheer' meant, but when it was followed by 'up' I was a bit lost! It was so nice. Dennis had a much bigger heart and was more sensitive than people realise, because of his public way of portraying himself. He was a very good captain.

"I would not say he was one of a kind, but I think Dennis was very good for the foreigners. When we came to London, we learned about newcomers having to stand up in the canteen and sing. Believe it or not, it happens everywhere in Europe now in football, and it's probably because of Dennis and Chelsea. All the foreigners at the club went back to their national teams and explained what they had to do, so it would come into the national squad when there were any newcomers. Dennis was just so good – he made us welcome, he set the rules and he was a captain able to pull together the British soul and the foreign soul of the side. We became like a proper team very quickly."

Vialli was afforded a two-minute cameo at the end of the 1997 FA Cup final, which many thought was his opportunity to say goodbye to the Chelsea supporters. It was the end of a glorious campaign for the club, but one of personal anguish for a player who had failed to live up to his illustrious reputation.

"I think Ruud was showing me respect there," Vialli says. "I think he probably felt I played a part in the FA Cup, in us getting to the final, and he felt this guy needed to play a little so he'd give me the satisfaction of being involved. From my point of view, I wasn't thinking about leaving. I don't remember thinking I needed to find another club. No – I wanted to come back and show them what I can do.

"The only time I thought about leaving was just before I became player-manager. I was playing more, but I was frustrated with the rotation system which didn't really make sense. You don't just think now how you want your side to play for the next five matches; if you change a player, it's because he's tired, not because you think he's going to get tired. Ruud's way of managing the four strikers – including Tore Andre Flo by then – I didn't particularly like it and I was frustrated, so I was thinking of maybe leaving. My friend Atillio Lombardo was at Crystal Palace and I thought about them, but also Celtic and Glasgow Rangers."

It's a good thing he had second thoughts, for it is as a manager that Vialli is best remembered at Stamford Bridge, and a very good one at that. At the age of 33, he took the reins from Gullit in controversial circumstances and went on to enjoy what was then the most successful reign of any Chelsea manager, winning five trophies.

The role of the player-manager was en vogue in English

football at the time, but since the turn of the century there have been only three in the English top flight, each of whom was appointed on an interim basis: Stuart McCall (Bradford City), Garry Monk (Swansea City) and Ryan Giggs (Manchester United). It takes more than 500 hours of theory and practical study to complete the UEFA A, B and Pro Licence badges, which is a lot for any player to fit into their schedule and goes some way to explaining why so few have been called upon in recent times.

"It's like being the director and the main actor at the same time," Vialli says. "You're wearing two different shoes all the time, always dealing with other stuff. It sucks away all the energy. I managed to do it reasonably well for a while, but then I realised it was either playing or managing. I couldn't carry on doing both.

"Having said that, when you are a player-manager it is great because you can test your methods on yourself. You come up with a training session that you think is great because it will help you to achieve a particular goal or objective. Then you finish the training session and you realise it was c**p and it didn't work! Or maybe physically it made you too tired, so you decide from tomorrow you're going to do less. It's really the greatest way to test your method until you find the right balance that works for you and the team. Then you can also feel the atmosphere on the pitch when you're playing the match – you can feel whether the players are collaborating, whether they work hard for each other, much better than if you're just watching from the sidelines shouting."

As much as Ken Bates derided the affection poured upon the Kings of the King's Road era Blues, in some ways it could be said he was following the example set from the Sixties or

Seventies, when young managers were handed the task of turning the club around. Tommy Docherty led the club to the League Cup in 1965, a few years after he had taken on the job as a 33-year-old with bags of charisma. When he surprisingly departed in 1967, the Blues appointed Dave Sexton as his replacement. A 37-year-old who had previously worked at the club as Doc's assistant, this well thought of coach and his slightly more pragmatic methodology helped take Chelsea up another notch, winning the FA Cup and European Cup Winners' Cup. He later fell out with several of his key players and despite the club initially backing him by selling fan favourites Peter Osgood and Alan Hudson, he eventually had to follow them through the exit door.

Fast forward to the Nineties and two even younger managers were entrusted with the managerial hotseat. The decision to replace the beloved Gullit was made all the easier by the affection the supporters had for Vialli, who they had taken to their hearts from the moment he arrived at the club and seemed to grow in conjunction with his deteriorating relationship with the Dutchman.

"I called Marcello Lippi, my old manager at Juventus, when the offer came in," Vialli recalls. "Obviously I wanted to just say yes and jump at the opportunity, but I needed to think about it because at that time I had no thought of becoming a manager. I was thinking of maybe going to the US, maybe into TV or something like that. Lippi just said, 'Do it! You'll be a natural.'"

But if Chelsea's plan was for continuity, they picked the wrong man for that. Where Gullit was all about sexy football and what we did while in possession, Vialli was a more pragmatic manager. He had been part of a Juventus side which employed a high press throughout their Champions League-winning year and the philosophy was almost as much about what you did without the ball than with it. He was a firm believer that a team was at its most vulnerable when it was in possession.

"When I look at the opposition, I think that way. I think it's easier for us to score goals when they have the ball. When they're in possession, they're going to set up in a way that they are building the offensive phase, so they spread, there is more space, and they are mentally thinking about playing the ball. If you are aggressive and you do it at the right place at the right time with the right energy, you can win the ball and they are not ready to defend. So, I am quite happy for a team to have the ball at the back and I can organise myself so that if I can win it back I can [clicks fingers].

"It's what Antonio Conte does, it's called transitions. It's what you do when they've got the ball and what you do when you win it back. Some teams win the ball, they pass the ball three or four times and then they look up. With Conte, they win it back, the first idea is to look up – the striker is already on the move and they can catch the opponents out and score goals. But at the same time, when I've got the ball I still want to do something with it, to build from the back and play effective, exciting football. It's about finding the right balance.

"As a manager, you start with the culture, the principles, the values, whatever you want to call it, and then you have the football principles. Then you've got your system and your tactics. The culture: I want to create a working environment where there is pride, humility and character. There is a meaning to what you do. I want to create an atmosphere that is so contagious, where the players wake up in the morning and they just can't wait to come to work. They feel like they are in the right place to become better players. Players worry about winning, money, but they also worry about being in a place which will make them better. That's what I wanted to create.

"Every manager has his own philosophy and way of doing things. I learned what Lippi thinks is essential in order to be successful; Giovanni Trapattoni was completely different; Vujadin Boskov was somewhere in between. Arrigo Sacchi was very influential to my way of looking at how the game was played, even though I didn't get on particularly well with him, but he was so knowledgable. You can then mould everything that you need to."

The environment Vialli created was a winning one, but all was not well in the camp during his time at the helm. Although it is only Frank Leboeuf and Dan Petrescu's account of the deteriorating relationship between players and manager that has been disclosed in the book, others also hinted at the disharmony which existed at the club.

Although Vialli was aware of unrest in the dressing room, the Italian says his eventual sacking still came as a shock.

"Maybe I was blind and I couldn't see that the players hated me, but I thought it was absolutely fine," he says. "Yes, Gianfranco wasn't particularly happy, or Frank Leboeuf or Roberto Di Matteo – but the latter wasn't my fault. He wasn't happy because he wasn't playing much and we had Jody Morris and also Didier Deschamps joining.

"The plan, which the club told me, was to sign Deschamps for free from Juventus and to sell Robbie for £3 million. Knowing Didier, who I played with at Juventus, and knowing Robbie, I thought it was quite a decent bit of business. I gave my approval. They ended up paying £3 million for Didier and not selling Robbie, so I had the problem of having too many players, which means unrest, which means unhappy players.

"Telling friends they are not in your plans was probably the most difficult thing to do. Not for the player-manager himself, because even though you worry when you get the job in the first place, after a while you realise you have to do it because it's for the good of the team. I was actually expecting, and I was wrong, more help from the players in order to help me do my job in the best possible way. I was a very young manager. Even though I was still playing. I was 33. I was expecting the likes of Desailly, Zola, Di Matteo, Deschamps, Dennis and everybody to understand I was doing my best but I needed them to help me. On the other hand, they were expecting me to help them because this is what the manager does. We were, in my opinion, very successful but not all the players were happy, they wanted more, or they were a bit confused to see me as one day their best mate, one of the chaps, and the next I am leaving them out, maybe affecting the future of them and their family. It's difficult."

When you consider the internal struggles within the camp, it is quite remarkable what the club managed to achieve in Vialli's two-and-a-half-years as manager. Prior to the modern era of success under Roman Abramovich, when winning has become a habit, it was the most successful period of the club's history and only José Mourinho has won more trophies as Chelsea boss. Not only was silverware lifted on a regular basis, we mounted a serious title challenge and finished third, only four points behind Manchester United's Treble winners in the 1998/99 season. Not good enough for Vialli.

"That was a huge disappointment. Huge. We were in contention almost until the last game of the season. The turning point, the crucial point – when the chips were down – was when we were playing Leicester at home. We were 2-0 up, I made a couple of substitutions and I was a bit disappointed by some of the attitudes of the players who came on, immaturity rather than not being professional. The coaches had been telling me to play myself in that match, but I couldn't because two days before I had to fly to Rome as part of the court case being instigated by Zdenek Zeman regarding Juventus and doping. I was so annoyed. Flying to Rome and back meant I missed training, I was tired, and I couldn't play myself. It's probably one of the reasons why we ended 2-2. I remember the equalising goal as well, the left-footed guy who cut onto his right foot. What was his name? Jippy? Gippy? Guppy!"

Disappointing as it was to miss out on the title, we finished in our best league position for nearly 30 years and, as a result, Champions League football was played at Stamford Bridge for the first time.

After the qualification round was successfully negotiated, the great AC Milan were the visitors to west London for our maiden outing in the group stage. Just a couple of years earlier, we had played the Rossoneri in a mid-season friendly at San Siro, and the prospect of a rematch in the biggest club competition of the lot seemed far flung at best.

"I bumped into some fans years later and they told me that game was the best 0-0 they ever experienced watching football. It was fantastic – it still gives me goosebumps thinking about it. We played that season as if we had always been in the Champions League, we had such authority and put in so many great performances. And then we were six minutes away from reaching the semi-final."

Barcelona were our quarter-final opponents and they were simply blown away by a scintillating Chelsea performance in the opening half which saw us lead 3-0 at the break. A vital away goal gave them hope for the second leg and at the Nou Camp they eventually prevailed 6-4 on aggregate and after extra time, although only a late goal from Dani forced the additional 30 minutes.

"The way I handled the half-time interval is one regret I have," he reflects. "It wasn't good enough. I was so upset. Sometimes I said what I felt instead of what I should have said, and that's what separates great managers from average ones. You always have to think about the repercussions of your words – it's not what you feel inside but what is useful for the players to hear. I wasn't good. Thank God, my assistant, Ray Wilkins, stepped up. It looked like we had worked out a strategy where I was the bad cop and he was the good cop! We went back in the second half, Tore Andre Flo made it 1-2 and we were much better in the second half. I was a bit let down, I shouldn't say this, by the attitude of two or three players, who were arguing with each other and being a bit childish, forgetting we were only this far away from history."

Had they seen the game out, could Chelsea have really gone all the way in our debut season instead of having to wait 12, at times torturous, years to finally get our hands on 'Old Big Ears'?

Vialli is unconvinced.

"Valencia played Barcelona in the semi-final and although they were not as good as them at playing football, they were very Italian in their style, very effective. I think they would have probably beaten us. Barcelona were great, but different – so we could beat them with our strategy. We were able to confuse them for 60 minutes in that first leg. Valencia played the game similar to us, but with slightly better players. They got to the final that season against Real Madrid and again a year later, so I'm not wrong in saying they were a very good team."

So too were Chelsea. A decade which started with a middle of the road, perennially underachieving side ended with a group of players who were giving the best in Europe a run for their money. And the supporters loved them dearly for that.

"I'm extremely proud. I don't boast about it. People ask, 'How many trophies did you win as a manager, one or two?' And I say to them, 'No, actually, I won five!'"

He laughs loudly at this statement, which included an expletive.

"I think I was the most successful manager at Chelsea until José arrived. The fans still remember me and they do it with fondness and respect, which is priceless. It was just so enjoyable. Looking back, I thought I did my best, I learned a lot and it was a great time for the club. I think the pillars were already there, but we finished building the first, second and third floor. Then there was a bit of a gap, but Roman arrived and they made a skyscraper. And one of the best. They're still adding floors all the time."

12. The Boss

'When you are the manager and you see all of a sudden you have control of the match and you have achieved your task, you get the moment to see the players' faces. You look at the crowd and see their faces. That was the best feeling I've ever had.'

"Ah, my lovely boy." Ruud Gullit has just walked into the canteen of our Cobham training ground to be greeted by a wide-eyed, grinning Eddie Newton. The two men embrace, just as they did on the Wembley turf 20 years ago, when the midfielder's late goal clinched the victory over Middlesbrough which meant the Dutchman became the first foreign manager to lift the FA Cup.

Soon they are catching up on the years which have gone by since they last met in Milan while Eddie was checking up on the progress of loan players Marco van Ginkel and Fernando Torres, reminiscing about the good old days. Gone are the dreadlocks, but none of the charm or charisma has left Gullit; within moments he is holding court as players flock to revel in the company of a living legend, a once-in-a-generation footballer who could genuinely lay claim to being the best player on the planet at one time or another.

While Newton and Gullit are now old friends, the scene of their reunion plays out in stark contrast to the latter's arrival at Harlington for his first day of training on a balmy summer's day in 1995, when football had yet to come home, sexy football was still a year away from conception and Chelsea still hadn't won a major trophy in 24 years. Eddie happily admits he was starstruck when he first came face-to-face with him – "Wisey had to pick my jaw up off the ground. I watched him from when I was a bubby, and now I was going to be playing alongside him" – but he was just reacting the same way as the rest of us when we heard the news that Chelsea were signing the great Ruud Gullit.

Let's be clear about one thing: Chelsea, prior to 1995, did not deal in world-class players. Very good footballers, yes, but you have to go back to Jimmy Greaves, a youth graduate, for the last player within our ranks who could even lay claim to being among the best in the business. Now, we had the man who had captained the Netherlands to the 1988 European Championship, won the Ballon d'Or the year before that, and lifted the European Cup in consecutive years while playing for an AC Milan team considered to be one of the all-time greats. It was a seismic shift in the Stamford Bridge landscape and one from which the club would never look back.

The childlike enthusiasm from the supporters at their club's sudden promotion to the back pages of the newspapers for all the right reasons was mirrored by the man who had lived with intense pressure throughout his playing career. For the first time in years, he was carefree.

"You must understand I came from Milanello [AC Milan's training ground], which was like you have now at Cobham," Gullit says. "Everything was modern for the time. To come to Harlington was like going back to my childhood, that's why it had its charm.

"It's like what you had as a kid – just a bench and some hooks, then you go to the showers – no fancy pantsy stuff, nothing. It was football without any responsibility. Just playing football. And I enjoyed the fact it was like that. I had been in a regime where you had to win. If there was a draw there was hell breaking loose. So it was work. I was working, really. You were being squeezed to get the best out of you every game.

"You also must understand that I was used to being followed by fans all the time in Italy. Fans there are very honest in their admiration and they touch you [pinches his cheeks] and they want to hug you. After a while, I just wanted to have my life a little bit back. So that's why I came to Chelsea."

Clearly, while strides were being made on the pitch to catch up with Manchester United at the top of the English football tree, and Ken Bates was doing his best to bring Stamford Bridge up to modern standards, there was still work to be done on the human relations side. Gullit's first days in England were not spent, as you may expect, living the high life in London. He was instead holed up in a hotel in Slough, along with fellow new signing Mark Hughes, and it wasn't until he plucked up the courage to drive on the left-hand side of the road – "The wrong side of the road," he says with a roar of laughter, shaking his head at the mere thought of it – that he first ventured into London.

"Then I took the car, which was a difficulty in itself, and I went to the King's Road. It was the only place I knew. I stopped there and I walked. At the beginning, I still had that attitude of being followed – you feel like the prey – and after 15 minutes I looked over my shoulder. Nobody is following me. That's nice! The first thing I did was go to a terrace somewhere. I sat there and just watched people for the first time in eight years. It was freedom. The best thing you can imagine. That's why I have to laugh at people who want to be famous. It has a lot of good things, but also a lot you wish would be different. So to be able to sit and relax, nobody coming to you, just sitting there, was the best thing that ever happened. It was exactly what I needed.

"I fell in love with London and I'm still in love with London. Look, I love Amsterdam, it is in my heart. But, for me, the best city in the world is London. I've been in New York, Milan, LA – I know. For me, London has everything."

It was a match made in heaven, for he was just what this football club needed. He was seen as aloof by those on the outside, which was partially down to his efforts to shelter his private life from public consumption, but from day one he was one of the boys and not above the banter within the dressing room. Ruud Gullit, superstar footballer, was reduced to the moniker of Big Nose by Dennis Wise and John Spencer. In return, they became his lovely boys as he channelled his inner-Windsor Davies, having been brought up on a diet of British comedy.

"The funny thing is, everyone was surprised I knew all the sitcoms – *Fawlty Towers, It Ain't Half Hot Mum, Love Thy Neighbour, Monty Python*. People couldn't understand I knew all these programmes, but I was also raised with them. So we have the same sense of humour and, for me, it was like coming back to what I was used to. I loved it. Look, I like a laugh, I like a banter, and I had all these crazy people around me. Nice, crazy people: Dennis Wise, Frank Sinclair, Michael Duberry, John Spencer and all the others. It was funny. We had so many funny characters, but good characters. Of course, it was a different level of football to what I was used to, but I felt great."

With Gullit in the side, it was as if someone had turned on the lights at Stamford Bridge; we had gone from monochrome to colour and the sound had been cranked up to 11. Chelsea supporters could hardly believe their eyes, and his all-round play was a cut above anything witnessed at the club for many a year. There was one pass against Coventry City which was out of this world, a 50-yard through-ball with the outside of his boot for Mark Hughes to score. The gulf in quality was on show, too, as Spencer fell over in an attempt to control the pass intended for the Welshman, who scrappily forced the ball underneath the keeper to score.

Perhaps his brilliance was best illustrated by a pair of goals he scored in his first season. The first, in a game against Southampton at the Dell, saw him stride forward purposefully before exchanging passes with Hughes and then nonchalantly dinking the ball into the back of the net and hurdling the goalkeeper in one fluid motion. The second, against Manchester City, merely highlighted the gulf in quality between him and the rest of his team-mates, as he waited and waited for something to open up and then, with no options developing, he jinked onto his right foot and unleashed a rocket which flew past the static goalkeeper.

It was a similar situation to what he had witnessed in the early days of his career with Feyenoord. Then, Johan Cruyff was the ageing superstar dictating the play, indicating to players where they need to stand, guiding them along. He also told Gullit he would need to learn to make others around him play better. At Chelsea, he undoubtedly did just that, but it quickly became apparent that he would need to adapt his game, too.

"I remember when I had to play sweeper early on," he recalls. "There's a long ball coming from the opposition and I can suss out that it's too high for the striker so I take the ball on my chest. And the crowd goes, 'Woooahhhh!' Then, I gave it to Michael Duberry. And Michael was like, what the hell! And he kicked the ball away. Glenn came to me and said, 'Ruud, I know what you do is right. But you can't do this here, because we're not used to playing like that. So can you please play midfield for us.' And that's what I did. It made sense. Normally, Michael would expect me to head the ball away, not to play it along at the back. That was the way things were done in England."

Soon he would have an opportunity to affect matters from the very top of the football club. Hoddle announced he would be leaving to take up the role of England manager, which was to be vacated after Euro '96 by Terry Venables. George Graham was the favourite to return to the club he had represented as a player in the Sixties, when he was known as Gorgeous George, but to this generation of Chelsea supporters he was the man who had helmed an era of '1-0 to the Arsenal' before his time at Highbury ended ignominiously when he was found guilty of receiving money as part of a transfer deal by a Football Association inquiry in 1995.

The fans let the powers that be know their thoughts on the matter during the final game of the season against Blackburn Rovers, imploring them to stick Graham where the sun doesn't shine. "We want Ruud," came the cries from the stands at Stamford Bridge. The fans had spoken, and the board wasted little time in acting, sending word for Gullit to come up and see them after the game. He claims it was the first he knew that he could be in the running to succeed Hoddle.

"That did me a lot of good and I appreciated it – most of all the trust from the fans," Gullit says. "But I had to think about it because it was difficult. I was still playing and I loved every minute of it when I played at Chelsea. With Milan it was a regime. Monday – training; Tuesday – training camp; Wednesday – Champions League; Thursday – come back to the training camp, evening at home; Friday – training; Saturday – training camp; Sunday – play. Then you come to England. Wednesday – off; Saturday evening – free to go to the cinema, you could go out with your friends, out to the restaurant, all kinds of nice things; Sunday – off! Can you believe this? I never had that in my life! Sunday off! I had the opportunity also to go and see my mum. She was sick, she had breast cancer, and I could go to Amsterdam on the last flight on a Saturday evening, stay with my mum, and Monday morning come back. That was unbelievable for me to stay with her.

"So, I really enjoyed playing again. The club still wanted me to play, but I knew if I was going to take it, I would not be playing. I did in the beginning but slowly, slowly I was taking myself out of it. The thing is, I knew exactly what I had to do as manager. I knew what I needed to strengthen the team, especially the spine. So I took it, and that's what I did – I tried to get all these players to strengthen the spine because I needed that to be right. It's like the spine of your body – if something is missing there, you collapse, you can't function."

Unlike the previous player-manager, whose managerial career had already begun with two years at Swindon Town, Gullit had no experience of the role to fall back on. It was a risk and also in the sense that he was, clearly, our best player. After his first season at the club he had finished second in the voting for the Football Writers' Association Footballer of the Year award and been selected as the pick of the bunch at Chelsea by the supporters. This was a player who was still operating on a higher plain to the rest.

The initial plan was to have him work alongside a senior figure. Sven-Goran Eriksson was approached, but the future England manager's expertise was coaching, not the all-encompassing management style favoured by Premier League clubs at the time. Instead, Colin Hutchinson was effectively working as the sporting director, pushing players in the direction of the new head coach, and Gullit would focus on training the squad.

When he took on the job, Gullit had a bigger job on his hands than merely bringing sexy football to Stamford Bridge.

For all of the improvements made under Hoddle behind the scenes and in changing the playing culture, he had been unable to instil a winning mentality in his group. In his final season at the helm, the club had failed to secure victory from a leading position on 17 occasions. But the new manager got his spine right over the summer, recruiting a defender, Frank Leboeuf, a midfielder, Roberto Di Matteo, and a striker, Gianluca Vialli.

Media interest in the Blues, according to the first matchday programme of the season, was "almost indescribable" ahead of his debut in the dugout against Southampton. That "as many as 50 people arrived" for the first press conference of the season, including camera crews from Holland, Norway, France and, of course, a large Italian presence, may seem like a drop in the ocean compared to today's media saturated football world. But two decades ago it was the big time like we hadn't known it for many a year before.

Gullit was preparing to take charge of his first competitive match as Blues manager, and it should be noted that the Saints had a former European Cup winner of their own at the helm, Graeme Souness. That was where the illustrious comparisons ended, though. Formation-wise, forward thinking 3-5-2 was playing prehistoric 4-4-2, while the individual battles across the pitch told another story of how Chelsea were setting a new agenda for English football: Leboeuf versus Neil Shipperley; Di Matteo battling against Barry Venison; Vialli looking to outwit Richard Dryden, fresh from a third-tier relegation battle with Bristol City. It was a different ball game. But not everyone was happy. Early on, there were rumblings in the press that the captain, Dennis Wise, was disillusioned with his new manager, who had seen fit to leave him out on occasion.

"He was convinced I wanted all the English out," Gullit

recalls. "That was his thing. Dennis was in those days still the Dennis Wise who wanted to play like the Crazy Gang. I didn't want that. I told him so many times: 'Don't do crazy things!' He kept getting yellow cards, whatever. We had a match against Leicester away, and we were 1-0 down. Dennis is again not listening, just doing his own thing. And I just, [clicks fingers], captain out. He went crazy. We won the match 3-1, so he couldn't say nothing. He was moaning to a mutual friend of ours, this guy we both played golf with: 'Ruudi wants only foreign players.' The guy said to him, 'No, that's not true, Dennis. I know that from Ruud. The best thing you can do is call him.' So he did, and I invited him to my house for dinner. I said, 'Dennis, look. I want you to forget the Crazy Gang, stupid tackles on people and red cards. I don't want that. You are an excellent player. I want you to play in the way I think you can. I will also tell you one thing: if you do this, you will go to the national team.' He was laughing at me! 'No, no, no. This is not to give you a good stimulant or whatever. This is what I believe. If you play like I think you need to play, you are my best player. And I ask you: can you do that for me? If you do that for me, you are my captain.' He looked at me and said, 'Okay, I'll do it.' And the rest is history.

"He became a far better player. A few years later he was in the national team, playing Champions League and not looking out of place. From that moment with me, he played unbelievably good. And not just because of me, but because of himself. He woke himself up. All I did was to say, 'This is what you have in you.'"

He has a similar story regarding Hughes, whose name he pronounces in a Dutch manner with a guttural sound on the G.

"Mark was unbelievable, but also with him I had an argument," he says. "Maybe not an argument, I just had advice. In the games in the beginning, he wanted to run into the corners, do this, do everything. I said, 'Mark, you see the width of the 18-yard box? I don't want you to come out of that width any more. You stay only in that width. I don't want you coming back, chasing players. No, we have other players. You are 33 years old, just stay in that area. That is your area. Nobody can take the ball off you.' He said, 'But that's what I've always done...' Yeah, when you were 26! Now you're 33. Only concentrate on that. 'Oh,' he said to me. Then when we were doing sprints in training, everybody had to do 10 and after seven I said, 'Okay Mark, go in and have a massage.' And of course he was happy! I didn't need only his energy, I needed his experience. When you are older, you don't need to train that hard any more. When you get older, you use that experience and when you see things you suss it out immediately. The older you get, your body doesn't want it any more. So therefore you need to adjust your body. Keep it in shape in a different way."

Gullit wanted his players to think about football more. He didn't like those who came to training, showered and then went home; he wanted a more cerebral approach from his players to find solutions on the pitch themselves rather than being micro-managed every step of the way. That was the Dutch influence.

"I just wanted them to think about their game and also the team. When I'm the manager, I want to know what they're thinking. I don't want any robots – a robot doesn't help me. On the pitch, things change. So when it changes, I need players who take responsibility on the pitch. I can scream however I like, but you need people with this inside."

It works both ways, too. If they were to take more responsibility on the pitch, they would also be afforded more leeway off it. For example, there was no curfew set on New Year's Eve despite the prospect of a game the next day at home to Liverpool.

"I wanted to give them responsibility," he explains. "It's the same thing I do with my kids also. If they don't want to eat, I say, 'Okay, you don't need to eat it. But you don't get anything else.' I let them walk away to think. You have to give them responsibility. I remember getting the players to do a test to find out which food or drink they are intolerant to. Most of the time, you just don't know because you're used to them. It turned out a couple of them were intolerant of yeast. Can you imagine the reaction: 'What, no beer? Are you crazy!' I said, 'Look, you know you're intolerant of them, you can do whatever you like. It's your life. I just want you to know these things. Maybe you can play better without it, but do whatever you like.' I reminded them that yeast is also in bread, it's not only beer!

"I also brought in a guy called Ted Troost [a psychologist and physiologist], someone I worked with throughout my career. Nowadays it's very common that players seek other help than only physios; they do it in golf, every sport. With football it was always this old fashioned way of like, 'Come on, roll up your sleeves and get on with it.' It's not that simple. In my days, I was always seeking something in order to be better. So I had all kinds of things and that's why I brought Ted in. A lot of players asked for his help."

Most of the players spoken to for this book have pinpointed the relaxed environment in which they operated as being a key part of their success.

"That's how I am. I had to laugh always about people who thought I was arrogant. Maybe it's because sometimes I try to protect myself, I don't want to show myself that much. But I'm very, very relaxed. The thing is, the players also need to know it's about something else, an end goal.

"If you win and you play well and everything, it's the biggest joy you have. You can't do it on your own. You need your players, everybody, around you. Not only the 11 playing, all the 22, you need them all, so I need you to have fun together. Good banter, but to be serious in the moment. Of course it's work, but you work so much better if you also enjoy what you're doing. And come on – who doesn't want to have this job? We're outside, playing football. What is not to enjoy about it?"

For all the good times, however, Gullit will never forget one of the saddest days in the club's history.

Vice-chairman Matthew Harding was travelling back from watching the Blues' League Cup match away at Bolton when his helicopter crashed on 22 October 1996, killing him as well as fellow passengers Ray Deane, Tony Burridge and John Bauldie, and pilot Mick Goss.

Our next match was at home to Tottenham. Before kick-off, Dennis Wise, Kevin Hitchcock and Steve Clarke had carried out a floral message which simply read: "Matthew RIP". Fittingly, it was presented in front of the recently-built North Stand which had just been named after the man who had helped fund it.

The Chelsea players then linked hands and stood, like everybody else in the ground, sombre and utterly noiseless during the minute's silence. Blues supporters showed their appreciation with a standing ovation for their Spurs counterparts. The outpouring of emotion transferred to the players, who put in a performance which Harding would have been proud of. In his first Premier League start as player-manager, Gullit turned back the years with a virtuoso display behind the front men and opened the scoring in the first half, with Chelsea going on to win 3-1.

"It was a strange moment [the Spurs game], almost as if we were not there," Gullit recalls. "It was like, you didn't have to do your best because there was some force helping you do what you had to do. There was a quietness about the game. A strange feeling."

Gullit pays tribute to the role Harding played in transforming the fortunes of the club.

"He believed in everything we were doing. Matthew was the starter of all of that, along with Ken Bates. He was more like a dreamer and I think his dreams came out. He had visions for how he wanted Chelsea to become. I cherish that I had the opportunity to meet him."

Although Gullit has turned his hand to management sporadically since his premature departure from the Stamford Bridge hotseat – and he looks all the younger for it, with scarcely a grey hair to show for his 54 years – one aspect he seems to miss is the psychology that comes with the role of leading a group of players.

Many of those who played under him noted how little focus there was on the opposition when it came to team talks, especially from a coach who had spent much of his playing career in Italy. The pre-match build-up to the FA Cup final featured very little on the Middlesbrough side we were coming up against and was centred largely on his own group of players and what they were capable of.

"That was because I was convinced we were much better," he explains. "So you have to show that attitude to the players. The best example of how to manipulate psychologically was the semi-final against Wimbledon. I knew they would be only trying to hit us, to provoke us, to kick us. The thing they hated the most was that they were playing at 'home' because the home locker room is the far end at Highbury and the away side are the ones close to the tunnel. They wanted to have us going past them, so they lost that already. I knew they were going to do something – and they put the ghetto blaster out there as loud as possible. We didn't care. I was thinking about what to do, so I said to my players, 'Look, go in the tunnel.' So we all went in the tunnel, and I stayed halfway and on their side. It's a very tight tunnel at Highbury and Wimbledon were coming and saying all sorts of things to try and intimidate us. I was just standing there and when I turned around there was Vinnie Jones."

It's worth interrupting at this stage to mention the history between the two men. The first time they crossed swords was in December 1995, when the Wimbledon hatchet man lunged in on Gullit and received the 11th red card of his career. He accused the Dutchman of diving and claimed his "pot-bellied pigs don't squeal as much as him".

"I said to him, 'Hey Vinnie, how you doing? Everything okay? How's your wife and kids and everything? I hope you have a good game.' And I did that with everybody. Later on I talked with... what was his name again? One of the Wimbledon players, nice guy, now works for NBC in America. Robbie Earle! He said, 'You effed us there so much.' I said, 'Yes, of course I knew what you were trying to do.' I told my players one thing: 'If they kick you, you all go there. All the players go there moaning about it, they get a yellow card, and then we're going to play football.' It happened exactly in front of me. Bang! Everybody there, referee gave a yellow card, and then we started to play football. I knew they'd try to provoke us, try to kick us. And it was a good team, Wimbledon, a very good team, because tactically they were well organised. I didn't underestimate them. I changed my tactics also, because we were playing 3-5-2 and I decided we were going to go four at the back. And they didn't expect it. When I mellowed them in the corridor, that was good."

When the big day came at Wembley, the opposing manager was Manchester United and England legend Bryan Robson. Both had taken a similar approach to the make-up of their squads by attempting to integrate foreign superstars into a predominantly British set-up, but while Chelsea's path was towards greatness, Middlesbrough were relegated and about to lose their second cup final of the season.

Instead of Robson becoming the latest Brit to lead a side to FA Cup glory, Gullit became the first foreign manager to lift the famous trophy, since when it has become the norm rather than the exception. Bar Harry Redknapp and Sir Alex Ferguson, every manager to subsequently win the competition has been from overseas. It was as gratifying an experience as winning the European Cup as a player.

"Of course it equalled it," Gullit says. "That was because I was a coach. I could see it from the outside and not the inside. When you're inside, you're still trying to do anything to win this game. When you are outside, and you see all of a sudden you have control of the match and you have achieved your task, you get the moment to see the players' faces. You look at the crowd and see their faces. That gives you an unbelievable feeling. That was the best feeling I've ever had. Because it's from a different perspective.

"Would I have liked to have been there with the team in my kit, kicking every ball with them? No. I was leading out a team at Wembley – that was the best. Come on, that was fantastic! I played at Wembley, I had that opportunity, but to go out there onto the pitch before the game in front of my team was fantastic. That's something they'll never take away from me."

As the players took the walk up the steps up at Wembley to receive their ultimate prize, one man was conspicuous by his absence.

"I was still down there watching them. I wanted to see their faces and also the fans. I was the happiest man in the world. I wanted to see them lift the trophy and I could say, 'Look, this is what you've done. Be proud of it.' It was just pure admiration of them. It is something I will never forget. That's why I was late going up there.

"I was just so proud of the boys. Robbie's first goal. So proud, as I was of Eddie Newton, because they'd blamed him for the loss in the other final, but then he came back and he could score the second goal. That was the icing on the cake, the best thing."

It looked to be merely the first chapter of a long career at the helm. Though the very nature of football tends to dictate that 'happily ever after' is rarely how the story ends, no one could have anticipated the speed with which Gullit was shunted out of the club just 10 months after leading us to a trophy which had been coveted for so long.

Second place in the league, League Cup semi-finalists and European Cup Winners' Cup quarter-finalists; now back-page news once again, this time for the wrong reasons, following the unceremonious dismissal of the manager after talks over a new contract broke down. The club said it was "unable to meet his demands" and that discussions had dragged on for too long, matters disputed by Gullit.

"It was a terrible feeling because it felt like an injustice," he says. "It was horrible."

All these years on, it remains a bitter pill to swallow, but remarkably it is the second time in the space of a week he has been asked about the circumstances surrounding his exit, having just discussed it on Italian TV with none other than the man who replaced him in the dugout.

"Luca was very honest when we spoke about it on TV. If somebody says to you, 'We are trying to negotiate a new contract with Ruud, but if it doesn't work do you want to be the coach?' Is that strange or not? At least you know already what you're doing. So then he was asked to go to the training ground and he thinks maybe they'll tell him Ruud has extended his contract.

"He was also surprised [at being offered the job]. That's why I said I didn't have it with Luca so much. I had it with other people. Sometimes, if you don't see it coming, it's like, 'Huh?' But I don't blame Luca."

13. Cup King

'One thing I can say about every game at
Chelsea was that I was never on my own,
there was always someone looking over
my shoulder. This is the feeling we had
in the dressing room. There was always
somebody there to fight for you.'

For the man who made his name doing something faster than anyone else, it is ironic that Roberto Di Matteo is running late for our chat. He has arranged to meet me in Chinoiserie, which is described as "the perfect place to sit and relax, gather with friends and family or host an informal meeting to the soothing sounds of our resident harpist", at the Jumeirah Carlton Tower located on Sloane Street in the heart of Knightsbridge. Swanky doesn't even come close to doing the place justice, for its decadence knows no bounds, and I feel underdressed for the occasion.

When he arrives a few minutes later than scheduled, my first feeling is relief. It's a familiar feeling as a sports writer, for whom being stood up is an all-too-regular occurrence, but on this occasion it is as much to do with what he is wearing; he's almost got the smart-casual look down to a tee, his shirt and jumper combo accompanied by jeans and a well-looked after pair of brown brogues.

The aforementioned harpist is in full flow as we take our seats at a table for two, and indeed throughout the 90 minutes I spend with Robbie. Background noise, as anyone who has recorded an interview will inform you, is a pain in the backside, but on this occasion it adds an ethereal soundtrack to the thoughtful and ponderous tales being relayed to me by a man who was front and centre in two of the biggest triumphs in the history of Chelsea Football Club. Although it is slightly surreal to hear him lamenting the morning paper round he undertook in the dead of winter as a young boy growing up in Switzerland while the harpist performs his best rendition of the Robbie Williams song *She's The One*.

As a member of the publications team at the club since the summer of 2008, there was a brief time that I could refer to

Di Matteo as a colleague, when he was the Blues' assistant first-team coach followed by an eight-month spell as manager, during which time we had crossed paths in the corridors of our Cobham training ground and polite pleasantries were exchanged. Professionalism always came out on top, but there were occasions when I wanted nothing more than to give him a big hug for providing this lifelong Chelsea supporter with moments of joy that were beyond my wildest dreams when I first began following the club in the early-Nineties. The 12-year-old me would be disgusted that I spurned such an opportunity.

Let's take a moment to briefly recount those moments. There are the three Wembley cup-final strikes; the first, a 30-yard thunderbolt after only 43 seconds, helped secure a first FA Cup triumph in 27 years; the second clinched a first League Cup for 33 years; and the third was the only goal of an otherwise forgettable last FA Cup final at the old Wembley Stadium.

He was already a bona fide Blues icon for his achievements on the pitch and it is almost forgotten that he also subsequently managed the club to FA Cup glory in 2012, because two weeks after that he delivered the big one, the Champions League. Twelve years after he had been part of the Chelsea side which made the club's first foray into elite continental competition, and after so many near misses and hard-luck stories, we could finally call ourselves champions of Europe.

My opening gambit is the million-dollar question: what is the defining image of Roberto Di Matteo at Chelsea? I speak for all Blues followers when I say the shortlist can be whittled down to two, but which comes first: the blockbuster, record-setting strike at Wembley and the jubilant celebration which followed, or the moment on the steps of the Allianz Arena in Munich, when he embraced with Roman Abramovich before screaming, "We did it," echoing the unbridled joy felt by Blues fans the world over?

"I think it's probably the FA Cup final in 1997," Di Matteo responds. "Actually, I'm not 100 per cent sure. What I noticed is that a lot of people would know the Champions League, but the true, loyal Chelsea fans would probably say 1997. For the general public it's probably 2012."

How nice it is to be confronted with such a quandary...

"It is. But I worked very hard for it!"

Didn't he just. It all stems back to his upbringing in Switzerland, where he was born and raised by his Italian parents, and the values of hard work were instilled in him from a young age. Although he claims to "only know football", he is a more well-rounded individual than he gives himself credit. In part, that is down to his experiences in the game – the highs and the lows, both of which he experienced at Chelsea as a player and a manager – but he got his BA diploma at school and undertook various different work placements, including as a butcher, a baker and a mechanic.

"I did many things for work experience in Switzerland, many different jobs," he remembers. "The worst was probably delivering the early papers. I did it from October till March. I got up at 5.30 in the morning, did my paper round, then went to school. It was an hour-and-a-half, freezing cold, always snowing."

Those newspapers would later regularly feature Di Matteo on the back pages. But for someone who made such a habit of hitting the back of the net in spectacular fashion, often on the big stage, goalscoring was not the forte of a man who once described midfield players as the ones who "invent the game", suggesting a more creative side.

Upon joining Chelsea, it quickly became apparent that he didn't seem to possess one outstanding quality as a midfield player, although that is not necessarily a weakness. As the matchday programme put it towards the end of his first season at the club: "You look at Robbie and you think there are better passers, better tacklers and better goalscorers, but then you think who has come out on top against him and you are struggling to count them on the fingers of one hand. He, more than any other player in our side, runs games. He sets the tempo with his ability to quicken or slow the game down."

A more succinct way of putting it, in modern football parlance, would be to say he was well-versed in game management. He'd learned his trade in Switzerland, winning a league championship with Aarau in a season which saw him crowned the country's Player of the Year, and played for Lazio in Serie A. He was an Italian international approaching the prime years of his career at the age of 26, and here he was signing for Chelsea. You can argue the importance of our signings in the mid-Nineties until you're blue in the face, for there is no right or wrong answer, but a strong case can be made for Di Matteo being perhaps the most significant of the lot. He was not a thirty-something coming over to England for one last adventure – or payday, depending on your level of cynicism – nor was he a virtual unknown like Frank Leboeuf, who claims he went unrecognised even in his homeland. This was a player costing us a club-record transfer fee of £4.9 million and, as he prepared to leave Rome, he was confronted by disgruntled Lazio supporters, such was their frustration at seeing one of their star men depart.

"They weren't happy that the club had accepted the offer from Chelsea," Di Matteo explains. "It wasn't a very pleasant experience. After this, they came to apologise because they realised it wasn't pleasant and it wasn't the way they should have reacted. It was hard for me, I was playing for a Lazio team which was fighting for titles and I was also appearing regularly for the national team, so it was a gamble for me to come to England. But I saw the influx of foreign players and I recognised that the Premiership was growing as a league. It was important that it was an ambitious club with good plans and ideas to move forward. The club made a big effort to sign me. That was the most important aspect for me.

"I don't think many people knew me as well as they did, say, Vialli, and I remember my introductory press conference was really low profile. I felt very comfortable with it; I knew Ruud wanted me at the club and they made a big investment in me, which I believe was a club record at the time. I knew it was the right place for me to go for my professional career and also for my personal life, too. I could just feel Ruud had confidence in me. I had a fantastic relationship with him and I probably played my best football with him. When you feel the confidence of your manager, you can express yourself and show the qualities you were bought for."

Straightaway, he knew he had chosen the right club and the right city, from the moment he first set foot in London.

"What I came into was very much a family environment," Di Matteo says. "Ken Bates and his wife, Suzannah, were the driving force behind that. It felt really homely to be part of the club and close to the chairman and his wife. They took me and my family for lunch one day, which the chairman in Italy would never do, so I just felt like I was in a big family.

Me and the other guys who came over tried our best to adapt as quickly as possible to the British culture and mentality, and it was a nice atmosphere.

"I didn't actually know much about London when I signed, I'd never been there before. Then, I remember when I came over for my medical, and I was picked up from the hotel on Cromwell Road. We were driving through Hyde Park and I just couldn't believe there was such a nice park in the middle of town. First of all, I was amazed at how big the city was, I just didn't realise, and how beautiful it was. And you've got this massive park in the middle of town, which was really pretty. I'd been brought up in Switzerland, where there was a lot of green, and I didn't realise such big parks could be in the middle of the city."

While Di Matteo smoothly settled into life in the capital, the odd mishap could perhaps be expected while he adjusted to his new environment.

"I was in the hotel for a couple of months after I signed and then, because I was committed, I bought an apartment flat near Hyde Park in South Kensington," he continues. "I was already sold on Hyde Park! It probably took me half an hour to Harlington and 10 minutes to Stamford Bridge, so it was perfect. Well, almost perfect. I've got a funny story...

"When I was staying at the hotel they had a parking area for my car, obviously, but when I moved into my flat, the first night I parked the car in front of the building. In Italy, you park your car in front of where you are living, it's normal. The next morning I came downstairs and my car was not there any more. Come on, I can't be that unlucky! It's not possible that the first night I am in my apartment someone has stolen my car. So I called the club and said, 'I'm very sorry but I'm going to be late for training because they stole my car.' What do you mean? Where did you park it? 'I parked it in front of the building where I live. I only moved in yesterday.' Do you have a residents' parking permit? 'A what? What is that?' Okay, so you need a parking permit to park your car in front of your building. Lesson learned!'

Di Matteo has lived in England for the majority of the past 21 years, aside from a brief spell in Italy when he retired from playing and a short stint as manager of Schalke. The first two of his three children were born here, the eldest of whom is 17 and a passionate golfer like his father, and his wife is a Londoner who is half Irish. She hasn't managed to turn him into a Guinness drinker yet.

He came over at the height of Cool Britannia and the nation had just been dazzled by football coming home at Euro 96 – although, in truth, without the rose-tinted glasses applied by England's run to the semi-finals, the competition was actually rather dull and workmanlike. It was the atmosphere in the stadiums, rather than the matches, which really stood out, and the effort to break away from the hooligan image which had haunted our game with a tournament that felt inclusive to all. Di Matteo was part of the Italy squad which failed to get out of the group stage under the great Arrigo Sacchi, but the experience whetted his appetite for English football.

"I really enjoyed playing here," he says. "The football stadiums were just magnificent. In Italy and Switzerland, many of the stadiums still had the running tracks around them, so seeing proper football stadiums and the atmosphere they generated was wonderful. I really liked the sport culture that existed in England. As long as the team gives everything and fights for each other, the fans would appreciate your effort. I think this is something that was a bit of an eye-opener for me, the way they showed a certain maturity of sporting culture that exists in England.

"We played our group games at Old Trafford and Anfield, so that was a really great experience for me before moving here. We were based up in Chester and didn't get out of the group because my small friend missed the penalty. He made up for it in the years that followed."

He is, of course, referring to Gianfranco Zola, whose subsequent arrival later in 1996 gave a whole new meaning to the beautiful game for not only Chelsea supporters, but followers of English football in general. That year it felt as if someone had pushed the reset button after the traumas which dogged our game for so long, and the Blues were leading the way with all of these exotic new overseas arrivals and the expansive football cultivated by the graceful hand of Gullit.

Of course, it's easier for Chelsea fans to think this way because of how the first season of the revolution concluded. And as much as Di Matteo would like to credit his small friend, he was one of the poster boys for the change. Before Zola was even so much as a consideration for the Blues, let alone playing for us, the club had ushered in a new era of cool thanks to an off-the-cuff celebration sparked by his compatriot.

When an early-season encounter with Middlesbrough was turned into a battle of the opposing former Juventus strikers, Gianluca Vialli and Fabrizio Ravanelli, it was left to another hero from the Apennine peninsula to break 86 minutes of stalemate with a low thunderbolt from 25 yards that whizzed into the bottom corner of the net in front of an empty Shed End, which resembled a building site in the early stages of the grand redevelopment of Stamford Bridge.

The shot was struck by the trusted right boot of Di Matteo, who dropped to the turf before raising his right arm in celebration. Following his lead, a number of team-mates expertly improvised, although a spread-eagled Frank Leboeuf rather spoiled the choreography. The papers lapped it up; west London was the only place to be and Di Matteo had announced himself to the rest of the league.

"I will be very honest with you – that celebration wasn't planned at all," he reveals. "I wasn't a player that would score 20 goals a season. I think I managed to score 10-plus when I was at Chelsea, but I wasn't coming with a background of scoring many goals. We didn't plan any of it. I slid down – I didn't slip – and I just put my arm up with a finger raised. And everybody followed. That picture showed where we wanted to go; the finger pointing up, it was our way to go up. I was well happy to have scored in the first home game and to win the game. It was a great way of thanking the club and Ruud for signing me."

Di Matteo was a regular on the scoresheet under his new manager, thanks in no small part to a subtle change in his position intended to make the most of his accurate, yet powerful, striking from distance. At Lazio, he had been used to playing deeper in the midfield, but at Chelsea the presence of Eddie Newton as the anchor man freed him up to play higher up the pitch. Never was the result more spectacular than in his first FA Cup final, an occasion he had witnessed many a time without quite grasping its significance.

"In Switzerland they didn't show many English matches, but the final was always the one they showed live," he recalls. "I always used to watch it. What I also remember was that there was always nice weather and nine times out of 10 it was a sunny day. When you were talking about English weather, a bit like Switzerland, you say it's always raining, but I always saw a nice and sunny day for the FA Cup final, a beautiful ground and a great atmosphere. The only thing I didn't quite realise was the importance of it until I got here."

The whole journey to Wembley was a rollercoaster of emotions; from the astonishing comeback against Liverpool to the back-and-forth with Leicester, followed by the relief of reaching the final against a Wimbledon side that had previously revelled in giving the foreign legion a black eye. Every step of the way the fans were saying the same thing: "Is this going to be our year?"

The sea of blue and the wall of noise which greeted the players before kick-off in the final let them know in no uncertain terms that there was no margin for error. You already know what happened next.

"To score so early was unexpected, I must say! Very unexpected. I was very happy to put us ahead, I felt over the moon. I shortly lost total connection with what the moment was, I just started running. I didn't even know where to run. Everyone was chasing me. It was just a fantastic feeling, I had goose pimples. The rest, as they say, is history. It was obviously an important game for us as a club after 26 years without a trophy."

That figure was not fed to him; he knows the numbers behind the club which has been a part of him for the past couple of decades. He also seems uneasy with the idea of basking in the glory of his record-setting strike, and I remind him of his post-match interview, when he seemed rather blasé while discussing the magnitude of what had just occurred.

"Wembley was a good pitch for me and 1997 was fantastic,

a wonderful experience," he reflects. "Certainly one of the best times I had in my career. But if I can say that it is because football is a team sport. It takes the effort of everybody involved, even those who maybe played less and those who didn't play: the kitman, the physio, all the masseurs. Without everybody being together and working towards an objective, you will not achieve anything. I managed to score the goal, which helped us massively, but it is a team effort. Defenders have to defend, strikers have to try to score the goals, midfielders have to do both. Everybody tries to do their job to achieve what you set out to achieve. And we had a great party together afterwards."

Even Pele, who had been a guest at the game, showed up in Mayfair to congratulate the players.

"That's right, Pele came to visit us. I had met him once before in Switzerland."

Does he think Pele told the other guests at the party he'd met Roberto Di Matteo once before?

A huge roar of laughter.

"I'm absolutely certain that he does! Come on, Pele is a legend. For you it would be like meeting with the Queen."

Di Matteo seemed to reserve his best moments for cup finals, scoring in each of the three he played at Wembley, but he also came alive in the derby matches. He scored three of his 26 goals for the club against Spurs, including one in the emotional haze of the first game after Matthew Harding's death, and he helped settle a League Cup semi-final versus Arsenal with a ferocious strike which perhaps rivals his effort against Middlesbrough as the best of his time at the club. As someone who had come from Lazio, he was well versed in passionate local rivalries, having regularly contested the Derby della Capitale against their neighbours Roma. He notes that

Paul Gascoigne will be forever remembered as a saint by Lazio supporters for scoring in the game, but it was something he was never able to achieve himself and you can hear the regret in his voice as he laments this fact.

By sheer weight of numbers, London derbies simply cannot incite the same level of passion as in a city where beating your rival is at the forefront of your objectives for the season. Instead, what Di Matteo discovered at Chelsea was a non-geographical rivalry where the hatred stemmed back to a brutal FA Cup final in 1970.

"Leeds is another story," he explains. "Games against Leeds, my goodness me. There seemed to be at least one sending off in every game. You could sense the feeling. They made us aware of the history and the rivalry between the clubs and obviously I knew about that Cup final. You can change every single player, but put those two teams on the pitch together...

"One thing I can say about every game at Chelsea was that I was never on my own, there was always someone looking over my shoulder. This is the feeling we had in the dressing room. There was always somebody there to fight for you. I think the managers who were in charge of our group were, of course, good managers, but they were actually lucky as well because we were a really easy team to manage. We got along, we understood each other very well and there was an element in that squad that is very difficult to find.

"We weren't all best friends outside, but when we were in the club, you knew that your team-mates, the majority of them, would fight for you if anything went wrong. There was this element that went above the professionalism that you have these days. That's why I say the managers were quite lucky to have players like we were at the time. I couldn't tell you the reason for it. Somehow there was this harmony that was above normal. It was definitely the best dressing room I was involved in during my career. It was well-mixed, well balanced, and that's very unique. There aren't many teams that have that."

He retains a keen "emotional attachment" with the players he shared a dressing room with, keeping in regular contact with a number of his old team-mates. On those rare occasions they all get together, it is just like old times – the same worn-out jokes – just a few more wrinkles. Zola is the one he sees more often than the rest and it is clear they share the same family values.

"Gianfranco's father has passed away now, but you could tell from speaking to him why his son is such a nice guy. And from his mother, too. They're a wonderful family. I was on holiday in Sardinia in 2014 and went to visit Gianfranco's mum in his birthplace of Oliena. She was 84 at the time, I think, living on her own. She was very happy we came to visit her and the village."

As time passed, Di Matteo's impact at the club lessened and though there was still the odd bright spark, the first chapter of his Chelsea story came to an end in harrowing circumstances in September 2000. Only a few months earlier he had been the Cup final hero once again, scoring the winner in the final FA Cup final to be played at the old Wembley Stadium. Now, in St Gallen's Espenmoos Stadium, only an hour's drive from where he had taken those first tentative steps as a professional at Schaffhausen, he was laid out on the turf with his left leg pointing in the wrong direction. Career over.

"There was a loud bang and I looked at my leg and it was just hanging there," Di Matteo vividly remembers. "I knew it was broken, but I didn't know it was that bad. It was a triple fracture, with all the soft tissue problems that come with that. I believe in fate, in destiny, and I guess my time was up. I had just turned 30 at the end of May.

"I had so many operations, around 10 in total, and it took a long time just to do normal things like walking and running. There came a point when I just realised I cannot reach the level that is required to play as a professional footballer. I tried very, very hard to come back. We did everything and I just couldn't play any more."

Di Matteo opens up on what one of the darkest periods of his life.

"It was 18 months after the injury that I made the decision after consulting with the doctor. Every day it was a struggle and you try to reach a point where you leave this behind, but you never reach this point. I didn't realise at the time when I retired just how much it affected me, it was only many, many years later. I went through depression, I lost confidence. Your life is taken away; your dream is taken away. I was lucky enough to live my dream but then suddenly it's someone waking you up in the middle of a dream and saying, 'Sorry, it's over now.' As a footballer, you envisage how you would like to retire one day. Instead you have to retire because of an injury. There was a lot to deal with. The dynamic of your life changes. It wasn't in my plan to retire early."

During his time in the treatment room, Di Matteo was a mere bystander as Claudio Ranieri dismantled the side which injected joy into Chelsea Football Club once more. One by one his mates headed out the exit door.

"He had a very difficult task," Di Matteo admits. "The majority of that team had been together for many, many years and it was a difficult task to start to bring in younger players to refresh and improve the team. These are experienced, established players we are talking about, and obviously some took it better than others. Now, I realise as a manager how tough his job was at the time. Having to deal with all the players who had been at the club for many years, some of the first names on the team sheet. It was a difficult task which he managed to navigate and pull through.

"Claudio is a wonderful human being, though. He kindly offered me the chance to walk the team out at the FA Cup final in Cardiff after my retirement. It was a great gesture from Claudio and from the club as well. I enjoyed the moment, but obviously not the result [Chelsea lost 2-0 to Arsenal]. I thought it was the end of my career as a manager!"

Di Matteo took some time out of the football limelight to embark on a Master of Business Administration degree course and complete his coaching badges, but he remained a regular at Stamford Bridge.

"I used to go to every home game at Chelsea and soon I got that fire in my belly again," he says. "I was open to what role I could have in football and then MK Dons came calling when I was working for Swiss TV at Euro 2008. I went through the interview process, I'd never had an interview before in football. Then I got the job and I accepted because I wanted to see if it would be something I like, something I would be good at. If you don't try, you'll never know.

"I asked Eddie Newton to be my assistant. We played together for many years and now we have worked together for many years, but I don't see him so much outside of football. With Eddie it is very much professional. When we played together we were probably closer because we were both running around in midfield like mad men. He was doing some work in the

Academy of Chelsea and over the years we did the UEFA B and a couple of the other badges together in England. You talk about football and we had a very similar philosophy and views on how a team should play football."

For someone who believes in destiny, it wasn't lost on Di Matteo that he was back leading Chelsea out in an FA Cup final 10 years and one day after that grand gesture by Ranieri and the club. On this occasion it was as manager, having taken the reins from Andre Villas-Boas only two months earlier – and, of course, the Blues emerged victorious. A fortnight later he had led us to the greatest triumph of them all, winning the Champions League in Bayern Munich's own backyard.

"The night before the final we showed the players a video of messages from family, loved ones, friends," he reveals. "It was just a little bit of a personal touch, but that removed a lot of tension and nervousness from the room. I remember that very well. It was a surprise for the team. As cool as everyone wants to be the night before a big game, you are a little bit tense. That was a little personal touch to show them everyone was with us.

"I can't remember why I did it. I just thought that behind the players, who spend a lot of time away from home, there is a wife, parents, always someone you leave behind. I just wanted to do something different. There were a few tears and it was funny as well.

"Munich is probably one of the highlights for me. It's one of the biggest achievements a manager can achieve in club football. For many players at Chelsea, they tried for so many years to reach that ultimate goal without managing to put their hands on the trophy. It was a culmination of many years of hard work. Before, when I said I believed in destiny and fate, somehow it just all came together and I was part of it, I directed it.

"But I don't feel I have reached the top as a manager. I always think you evolve as a person, you learn something new every day. I'm not even sure where the top is. Where does it end? I don't feel like I have reached the goal. There is always something beyond that, something better or more exciting. There isn't an end goal in football management. There's always another target. Win one league? You want to win it twice or three times in a row. You want to win the Treble. Nobody has ever managed to win all four trophies. There is always more you can achieve."

Is the pressure you feel as a manager comparable to anything you experienced as a footballer?

"No, with a capital N and a capital O. The responsibility is all with the manager. As a player, you can share it with your team-mates – the enjoyment of the win or the pain of defeat. As a manager it's just yourself. You carry all the responsibility. It's two completely different jobs, if you want to call it a job as a football player, which I suppose it still is. One has not much to do with the other. The experience you gain as a player will help you to be a manager, but being a manager is completely different. For me, it's completely detached from being a footballer player, which is more enjoyable. No doubt about it. Nothing compares to running onto the pitch with another 10 team-mates, being able to influence the game and to be part of a winning team and the group environment and so on. It's a dream job."

The interview comes to an abrupt conclusion when his wife arrives at the hotel to meet him for dinner. I show her a picture of Di Matteo in his pomp, wearing a pair of sunglasses that should never have seen the light of day. She ignores the fashion disaster to rib her follicly challenged husband: "He wishes he still had hair like that..."

"No," he bashfully responds in a fashion none to dissimilar to that of a teenage boy embarrassed in front of a girl he fancies, casting a playful glare in my direction swiftly followed by a cheeky grin after his wife has turned to leave.

Football fans build their heroes up to be deities and we expect the world from them. Sometimes it helps to remember they are only human after all.

The Other Two

The Blues' FA Cup final squad also included defender Andy Myers and goalkeeper Kevin Hitchcock. They may not have made it onto the pitch at Wembley but both played a role during an important period in the club's history. In these interviews with Chelsea magazine, they opened up about the highs and lows of their respective careers....

ANDY MYERS

Having played for Chelsea and then returned here as an Academy coach [before moving to Vitesse Arnhem], how big a part has this club played in your career?

Chelsea have played a massive part in my career. I started here as a schoolboy and I went through the ranks. Back then it was the centre of excellence rather than the academy process but it was all along the same lines. I signed at the age of 12, then from the ages of 14 to 16 I went to Lilleshall centre of excellence and when I came back it was to try and get into the youth team. Eddie Newton and Frank Sinclair were a couple of years older than me and back then there was a group of young players trying to break into the first team. I was lucky enough to get my opportunity at 17, under Bobby Campbell, when I was

253

asked to come on as sub against Luton Town in the Old First Division in April 1991. We came back to draw 3-3 that day after being 3-0 down and getting booed off at half-time! My first goal came the next season in a 2-2 draw against Liverpool, under Ian Porterfield, and that was a massive shock as well, because I didn't expect to be playing.

It was great because you had Graham Stuart, Eddie Newton, Frank Sinclair, Damian Matthew, David Lee, Jason Cundy, Ian Pearce. They had all gone through the ranks and broken into the team.

Tell us a bit about your two years at Lilleshall, which younger readers may not know was the national centre of excellence run by the FA in the Eighties and Nineties for promising young players in England.

It was a big thing back then. You would go on all these trials and then you'd go away for two years to stay at Lilleshall. I was going out of London and out of my comfort zone for the first time and it was sort of like a boarding school, but with football every day.

The best thing about being there was having one of the greats of the game, Dave Sexton, coaching me for a year. The things I learned from him and his training – he was beyond his time as a coach. His enthusiasm for the game was unbelievable and you could tell he still had a love for Chelsea Football Club from when he was manager here because, me being Chelsea, he'd always look after me, speak to me and give me little bits of advice. I think the other boys even noticed that at times because I was the only boy from Chelsea in that year group! But he was unbelievable as a coach and as a person.

Your Chelsea playing career spanned the 1990s and there were major changes in the set-up at the club and also in expectations during that time. What did you feel was the biggest moment in that transformation?

The biggest change for me was when Glenn Hoddle came in. He wanted to play a different way, he thought about different systems like the 3-5-2 and he wanted get it down and play. What he actually did, without being too disrespectful to the other managers, is get hold of the actual individuals and develop them, especially the youngsters.

When you broke into the team at 17 in those days it was a little bit like, "Right, you're in. Learn." If you had injuries in that time your development stopped, and I had a few injuries. Going into the first season when I would have started, I cracked my ankle and tried to carry on playing over the next three years without realising it. There was a bone cracked in my ankle! When Glenn came in, it got sorted out. He just said, "Something's not right with this boy, he's limping. Something's wrong with his ankle."

When I got back fit, he knew what he wanted from you, as an individual, to help the team. So it'd be like, "Don't try that…give it here…defend that…bam." He knew what your strengths were and worked on them, but he wanted to work on your weaknesses as well. He took that time out to plan individual sessions and that was the biggest change I noticed. Then the food, the culture and the way we played all followed.

He knew what he wanted from his players and he got the best out of them, then the players he brought in elevated Chelsea to another level and we became fashionable.

When Ruud Gullit became manager in 1996, he brought some top-class players in, many of them from overseas, but there remained a group of Londoners in the side. Was that just the right blend at the time?

Yeah, I think it worked. One thing you can say about the players who came through the ranks is that we'd never give 100 per cent, we'd give more. We'd run through brick walls and do everything we possibly could, even when we weren't having the best of games. You could see that we cared. I think Ruud sensed that as well because it was our club, and when it's your club it means something to you. All the youngsters that were coming through after us, like Jody Morris, Michael Duberry and John Terry, you could see it was the same for them.

With that, and then bringing in the players he wanted as well, Ruud knew he had something. The new players got to learn what it meant to play for Chelsea because of that blend, and you could see how the club grew on all the foreign players who came in: Luca Vialli, Dan Petrescu. All of a sudden it meant something and everyone's on the same song sheet, driving to get success, pushing for cups and titles.

Did you learn a lot from Gullit?

Yeah, I learned from Ruud. I think I learned more from Glenn if I'm honest, but Ruudi took on what Glenn had done and he knew the attributes that we had and the way he wanted to play. He took me out from left centre-back to left wing-back from time to time, for example. But how could you not learn from someone like Ruudi? Even just watching him when he was playing for us, he was awesome as a player and awesome in training.

When he became manager, you knew he could do all the things that he wanted you to do, so he could back it up. If he was telling you to do something, he'd demonstrate it. It was the same with Glenn. You'd watch them do it and go, "Right...OK!" You're trying to learn and be as good as they are, but at the same time you're thinking, "Wow." You do get amazed.

Ruud's physical strength and what he did on the ball, that's what made him European Footballer of the Year and a world-class talent.

You played alongside some great defenders in your time at Chelsea...

Exactly, and to be fair that only helped me when I left the club to go and play elsewhere. When you're playing alongside players like that: Frank Leboeuf, a great reader of the game. David Lee, what a passer. Doobs had the pace to mop up and defend. Ruudi played sweeper at times as well. So, for me, that little spell I had playing in the back three was a big transition. I had to learn. When I was a kid, I was central midfield or left-wing, I never played full-back. My first game at full-back was against Matt Le Tissier in a first-team game against Southampton because Tommy Boyd was injured. Because I did well, I was played there again and suddenly I had to learn how to play full-back very quickly! This is the thing with football. You do anything you're told just to play for the club that you want to play for. You make mistakes, but you're learning.

Then we went to a back three and my position changed again, but when you're playing next to people like Leboeuf, Marcel Desailly and Paul Elliott before them, it gets you through it. You listen and you learn. When you look at some of the people I played alongside, you are talking about unbelievable talent.

In the end, did you move on to Bradford in 1999 because you wanted to play every week?

There were times under Glenn where he had said, "Look, I think it's time for a change for you" and I was training with the reserves at one point. Then I got back into the team, which can happen if you're training well. I got a run of games and then Glenn went. Then another manager comes in and I managed to get in the team under Ruud. Then Luca comes in and it's the same again!

I think there was a point where I looked at the players that were coming in and I knew. I needed to further my career and that's when I moved on. Did I want to move on? I had to for myself. Of course you don't want to leave the club that you were born to play for, the club that brought you through, but football doesn't work that way.

You returned as a coach in the Academy in recent years, re-establishing your connection with Chelsea. How did that come about?

When I finished playing in 2005, it was more a case of retiring due to injury. I had a prolapsed disc in my back and after that I lost power in my ankle, so it wasn't the same.

After that I was coaching my boy's team in Sunday League

and Bob Orsborn [from the Chelsea Academy], who had brought me to the club as a player when he was my school-teacher, asked me what I was doing. I said, "I'm just doing a bit of coaching" and he said, "Ah, come in!"

So after a year of coaching in Sunday League I went in to do summer camp at Chelsea under Neil Bath and Jim Fraser in 2010, and what I saw blew me away, in terms of what they were trying to do.

They gave me an opportunity – just part-time initially – and I was enjoying it so much taking training on Tuesdays and Thursdays, with games at the weekend. I was just loving it. It just went from there.

Did you develop a lot as a coach after returning?

Massively. I was coaching the Under-10s when I first came and I've worked with all the age groups as we were trying to work out where I'd best fit in. I worked with Joe Edwards when he was Under-14s coach, then moved up from there to the Under-21s. You have got to adapt to all ages and come down to thinking how the kids think at that age and what gets them into it. You've got to sort of go back to being a kid, then you've got to change and come back to being an adult again quickly when you need to be more disciplined and strict! At Under-21s level, you're trying to prepare them for going out on loan, so there's different challenges at all age groups.

In terms of my learning, I have been lucky to work with people like Joe, Dermot Drummy, Ian Howell and obviously Adi Viveash. You can only learn from coaches like that but you've got to be true to who you are as well.

KEVIN HITCHCOCK

You spent 13 years at Chelsea between 1988 and 2001, but it could have been even longer if the club hadn't rejected you as a youngster...

I was told I was too small and I would never be big enough to be a goalkeeper. To be honest, it wasn't until I left school that I really began to grow and fill out, and I was turned down by Chelsea before that. Then I got a job as an apprentice electrician and I played non-league football for two years, which was the best thing I ever did. I learned football by playing it. That sounds very strange, so I hope you know what I mean! I had to grow up very quickly, because the lower you go, the harder it gets. Especially for goalkeepers – we had to look after ourselves a lot more in those days. I had two years at Barking, near West Ham, and I was picked up by a top manager: Brian Clough.

He wasn't a bad judge of player, was he?

He was fantastic with me and I can remember the first reserve-team game I played for Nottingham Forest, which was up at Bolton and it was quite frosty. It was 0-0 at half-time and as I was about to run out for the second half, he pulled me to one side and punched me on the arm. "Young man, you're in this team because you're good enough. Now go out there and show me what you can do." I felt 10 foot tall. It was brilliant.

Unfortunately, it didn't really work out for me with Forest and I ended up at Mansfield Town, which is just up the road from Nottingham. I had a manager there called Ian Greaves, who was probably the biggest influence on my career. He was fantastic; a man's man, he looked after me, gave me my chance and I think I repaid his kindness and belief in me. I had four fantastic years there and then I ended up at Chelsea.

The club you joined in 1988 bore little resemblance to the one you departed in 2001.

I truly believe that Glenn Hoddle should take so much of the credit for the club Chelsea has become. He changed it, he made it professional. It was all in the details. He turned a terrible training ground into an average one. He made the difference with the players he brought in, he changed our diet, the philosophy of the football – everything. I couldn't give him enough credit for what he did for this football club and I was very sad when he left.

Now I can see why all the players used to joke that Hoddle was your dad!

Yeah, they did! It goes back to before he became our manager, I think it was around 1990/91. I'd just done my cruciate and I was out for a long time, and Glenn had come back to England from Monaco and he was rehabbing at Chelsea. We'd be working together at the training ground and then in the afternoon we'd go over to Stamford Bridge and we'd do rehab there. He was a legendary player and after he got fit, he went to Swindon to become their player-manager for a couple of years. During that time, David Webb came in as our manager and he sent me on loan to West Ham. I thought that was my Chelsea career finished, but Glenn came back as manager – and everything changed.

You played some of your best football under him, too. Do any moments in particular stand out?

It's so hard to pick just one. I always seemed to do well against Manchester City and I had a couple of great games at Maine Road. I think one match that really sticks out is going away to Brugge in the Cup Winners' Cup. I played really well and in those days we used to get the same flight as the supporters; we got on the plane and they gave me a standing ovation. That was unbelievable, it's something that always sticks in my mind. We beat them in a great game back at the Bridge and then went on to play Zaragoza in the semi-final. As good as they were, we were bad. But we signed Gus Poyet a couple of years later off the back of those games.

A lot of your time at Chelsea was spent as a back-up. Describe that role.

It was frustrating, because you just want to play. I worked with Dmitri Kharine, Dave Beasant, Ed de Goey and many more, and if I wasn't playing, I'd give those other keepers every ounce of my knowledge to help them prepare for the game at the weekend. I was desperate for them to do well. I'd give my all in every session to push them on. Whenever I speak with my young goalkeepers now ahead of a small-sided game in training, I tell them: "Make sure you're better than the guy up the other end." I pushed Bes and Dmitri, but not so much Ed – that was towards the end of my career – and I made sure they had to be on their toes. I'd like to think when I did come in and play for the club, I never let anyone down.

Did you have a good relationship with the other keepers?

Yeah, fantastic. Me and Bes were really close and it was tough when he had his problems with Ian Porterfield because I felt he was really, really hard done by. But we stuck together and I was one of the first to speak to him after that Norwich game, when the manager said he'd never play for the club again. Our friendship never wavered regardless of what happened on the pitch. I've never had an issue with another goalkeeper at Chelsea, we were always close and I was never jealous of anyone – if they played, I always wanted them to do well. Maybe that was one of my strengths.

The bond seemed to spread through the camp – it was a very tight-knit group.

I tell you who should get a lot of credit for that: Dennis Wise, Steve Clarke and myself. We were the senior players of the group and everyone who came in was told: "This is how we do it here. It's our club." And they all bought into it. We had people coming in after so much success in their career, but they all did it our way. Everybody was part of the family and that includes all of the people behind the scenes. When I go back to the club, there are still people here who were there when I started in 1988. It's a fantastic club.

You managed to survive around three different eras at the club, which took some doing.

I left in 2001 so I just missed the next era under Claudio

Ranieri, which was when the older players started to go. But the best thing was that someone was there to carry it on: JT. He kept going with what we built, which is amazing really, and he took it to another level. And I love him to death. He's done a great job – probably better than Wisey, but just don't tell him that! Make sure you put that I took good care of him. And I still do.

Did you know he was going to make it to the very top from a young age?

It's easy saying it now, but I used to say to him: "You're going to be as good as Tony Adams and Bobby Moore rolled into one." He just laughed! Every day I would terrorise him and his mate Nicho [Paul Nicholls], who was a young goalkeeper at the club. We had a lot of fun and they were really good boys who I wanted to look after. And John deserves everything he has got out of the game because he has worked so hard.

And we're not far off the 30th anniversary of your debut for the club.

I count myself very lucky to have played here. My career could have been better, but I did my best and I always enjoyed it. All these friendships I've made, all these memories.

FA Cup Final Match Report

Sunday Mirror, 18 May 1997

By David Barnes

Blue what a scorcher!

Chelsea 2-0 Middlesbrough
Di Matteo 1'
Newton 83'

Roberto Di Matteo grabbed the royal blue flag of Chelsea and flew it as high as their anthem demands.

He knows as well as the rest of this rich cosmopolitan gathering that Wembley has seen far more compelling matches in its time.

But never an FA Cup final with a quicker goal as the one Di Matteo struck to give Chelsea the lead after just 43 seconds.

Nor one that made Mark Hughes the first man this century to acquire four winners medals.

And not too many with the level of personal triumph achieved by unsung hero Eddie Newton who scored the second goal just seven minutes from time.

Newton, out of action almost all of last year through injury, felt his days at Stamford Bridge were numbered when Di Matteo signed for a club record £4.9 million fee.

Now they shared together Chelsea's most delirious domestic achievement since the Blues won the FA Cup for the first and only previous time 27 years ago.

Their exploits left Middlesbrough manager Bryan Robson, who has had so much glory himself at Wembley, empty-handed and full of all-consuming despair.

If Boro had a hope, then it lay with Fabrizio Ravanelli, scorer of 31 goals this season, lasting the 90 minutes. But his troublesome thigh forced him out of the action midway through the first half.

Robson's plight was to be pitied, but I have witnessed nothing more moving at this stadium than Concetta Di Matteo, Roberto's lovely blind sister, LISTENING to the sounds of her brother's success in the stand.

Her father, relating events at her shoulder, will not have known his son's opening goal beat by just two seconds one registered by Wor Jackie Milburn against Manchester City 42 years ago.

Di Matteo's shooting power was destructive but Boro suffered also from the rapier-like artistry of his passing.

There was not a rival to get within tackling distance of him for the Man of the Match trophy. No, not even Gianfranco Zola. Footballer of the Year, maybe, but he was a man searching for his genius here.

Nor Juninho, the Brazilian waif who has wept buckets of tears during a nightmare finale to a season that started with such blazing promise. Juninho's heart has appeared to be impossibly large within his tiny frame while he has battled to rescue something from the dregs of a broken season.

He did his best to leave Boro with the FA Cup as an enduring memory of his quicksilver talents.

And he certainly troubled Chelsea. Di Matteo could easily have been sent off rather than just booked when he brought the Brazilian down in the 55th minute.

You can imagine how Boro must have felt losing the Coca-Cola Cup final and dropping out of the Premiership through three docked points. But to go down to the fastest goal in any of the previous 115 versions of this showpiece was something else again.

It was a strike the speed and violence of which stunned the senses. Robbie Mustoe, overawed by the occasion, was mercifully withdrawn from Boro's midfield after just 28 minutes. Sadly for Mustoe, his first touch allowed Dennis Wise to slip the ball to Di Matteo.

Running straight at the heart of Boro's defence, Di Matteo made almost 50 yards before belting a 25-yarder over keeper Ben Roberts and in off the underside of the bar.

Di Matteo had approached the final deep within the shadows of men like Zola and Juninho. Both were considered to carry the greater menace in their boots.

But, perhaps inspired by the majestic figure of his manager Ruud Gullit striding on to the Wembley turf, Di Matteo was imperious.

One deft pass with the outside of his foot gave Scott Minto a chance to add to the lead on nine minutes.

Minto forced the ball beyond the challenge of Roberts. Skipper Nigel Pearson slipped in the act of clearing and Phil Stamp whacked the ball away from the empty net. Di Matteo's ruthless passing cut Boro to shreds once again halfway through the first half.

This time Romanian Dan Petrescu hoisted a lob over Roberts and was deprived by a courageous header from Pearson inches from the upright.

Boro lost Ravanelli within seconds of the incident. They must have sent him out to play with all fingers crossed and a prayer on their lips. For Ravanelli pulled up short after a challenge from keeper Frode Grodas signalled the end of his Cup final and, surely, his career with Middlesbrough.

He was replaced by Danish striker Mikkel Beck, but much of the passion and creative instincts vanished with him.

Gullit, tired of the tedious rhythms that invaded the game, strode to the touchline to demand that his team raise the tempo.

Zola almost responded with a thumping 30-yard free kick. But young Roberts, third choice keeper at start of the season, plunged sharply to his left to produce a save to treasure.

And soon afterwards only a linesman's flag for offside robbed Gianluca Festa of an equaliser.

Festa was furious to see his powerful header from Stamp's cross ruled out, but TV replays showed the decision to be correct.

Zola then played a crucial part in Chelsea's second goal as the clock wound down.

Petrescu lifted the ball beyond the far post. It would have run harmlessly out of play but for a clever back-heel from Zola that left Newton with a simple tap-in.

Zola had produced a piece of pure magic in the 71st minute when he evaded three challengers, turned inside, hurdled two more and fired a shot that Roberts saved - partly with his face.

Yet Chelsea fans still howled for the presence of Gianluca Vialli for whom they have such affection.

Vialli had asked Gullit to give him five minutes so he could carry the memory of Wembley into a fast approaching retirement. Gullit, apparently unmoved in the relentless quest for success, softened his heart and introduced him in place of Zola.

Concetta Di Matteo will not have understood the crescendo of booing Boro fans directed at FA chiefs Keith Wiseman and Graham Kelly before the start.

Nor their deafening clamour for those lost three points that have doomed them to relegation.

But she will always feel the full warmth of her brother's enchanting date with destiny.

Surely no one in the seats around her can have observed her sightless joy without having tears in their own eyes.

Thanks

Firstly, I cannot thank the players enough – not only for providing me with some of my fondest memories as a Chelsea supporter and giving me a reason to write this book, but for taking time out of their busy schedules to speak with me. Never meet your heroes? Nonsense. It was a pleasure speaking with each and every one of them, and I hope I have done justice to their words and actions.

Thanks to all at Trinity Mirror Sport Media. The cover and illustrations at the beginning of each chapter were produced by the talented Ben Renshaw, and Harri Aston's editing skills have helped sharpen up the finished product.

My colleagues in the Communications department at Chelsea are probably sick and tired of hearing about the book, but their support, knowledge and, perhaps most crucially, their extensive contacts books have proved invaluable. Thanks, in particular, to Emma Wilkinson, David Antill, Dominic Bliss – whose interview with Andy Myers appears at the end of the book – Rupert Cane, Thresa Conneely, Andy Jones, Paul Mason, James Sugrue and Richard Wilson. I am so grateful to be part of this wonderful team.

Thank you to Suggs not only for his sharp and witty foreword, but for giving us an FA Cup final song which has stood the test of time and acts as the perfect title for this book; just the mention of *Blue Day* transports me, and I am sure many other Chelsea supporters, back to Wembley 20 years ago.

When times have been tough, my friend and former colleague Garry Hayes has always been on the other end of a phone to offer advice and encouragement. It's unlikely I'd have written this book had it not been for first Steve Mackenzie and then John D Taylor giving me a chance and encouraging me to pursue my writing dream. Thank you for everything.

As Dennis Wise put it: "The people around you go through all this with you – the good times, the pain, the lot – and they need to share it with you as well and be part of it." A huge thank you, then, to my family: my mum, Pauline, brother, Nick, sister-in-law, Sinead and, most of all, my partner Hannah. I said after my last book that I was looking forward to spending more time with you all and less time glued to a laptop, and this time I mean it!

Initially, this book was going to be dedicated to my father, who is sadly no longer with us. Twenty-five years ago you chose to save me from a lifetime of misery by giving me a Chelsea kit rather than the strip of your beloved Aston Villa; I wish you were here now to see where that decision has taken me and I know you would be incredibly proud. We all miss you very much.

However, my life changed forever on Thursday 20 April when my son, Thomas, timed his arrival into this world impeccably – eight days early – to coincide with the book's print deadline. I've wanted to see my name on the cover of a book since I was a little boy and I was convinced this would be my greatest achievement in life, but then you came along to prove me wrong. This book is dedicated to you. Here is to a lifetime of happiness.

Richard Godden, April 2017